Divine Peace

Psalms
29:11

m

Divine Peace
ISBN 978-1-939570-17-8
Copyright © 1996, 2013 Mike Keyes, Sr.

Mike Keyes Ministries International
P.O. Box 91916
Tucson, Arizona 85752-1916
www.mkmi.org

First edition published 1996. Second edition 2013.

Published by Word & Spirit Publishing
P.O. Box 701403
Tulsa, Oklahoma 74133

Divine Peace

by
Rev. Mike Keyes, Sr.

*And the L*ORD *spoke to Moses, saying: "Speak to Aaron and his sons, saying, 'This is the way you shall bless the children of Israel. Say to them:*

*"The L*ORD *bless you and keep you;*

*The L*ORD *make His face shine upon you,*

And be gracious to you;

*The L*ORD *lift up His countenance upon you,*

And give you peace."'

"So they shall put My name on the children of Israel, and I will bless them."

—NUMBERS 6:22-27

My son, do not forget my law,
But let your heart keep my commands;

For length of days and long life
And peace they will add to you.

—PROVERBS 3:1-2

CONTENTS

Introduction

He has redeemed my soul in peace from the battle that was against me. For there were many against me.

—PSALM 55:18

In these last days, two things are going to happen. First, God will move on the earth like never before, working through His children to lead millions to Jesus Christ through signs, wonders, and mighty deeds. Second, the devil will attack the church like never before because he knows his time on earth is short. As these things happen, I believe it's imperative for believers to understand the power of God's peace.

This verse in Psalms tells us that, through peace, God promises to redeem our souls from the battles we face. There are four things to notice in this verse. First, David declared his faith in God—not just to deliver him from that one particular battle, but from every other battle he fights as well. It is going to be the same for us in these last days, so get ready—there are going to be many battles to fight, and they're going to be far more severe than anything we've faced to date on this planet, in this generation. In December 2007, the "Great Recession" began, and depending upon who you talk to, or what article you read, it ended anywhere between 2009 and 2012, yet many believe it hasn't really ended at all—the way it changed our way of life has still lingered on, and may be felt for many more years to come. Well, no matter where you are in that debate, I can say without hesitation that the worldwide chaos and confusion will be much worse in the near future, because Jesus Himself prophesied it would happen.

In Luke 21:25-26, Jesus warned us that just before His return, men's hearts would be failing them from fear, and from the expectation of things happening on the earth. He said the nations of the world would be in distress and perplexity; which means they're trying, but unable to solve the complex problems they face financially, economically, socially, politically, militarily, and religiously. When Jesus talks about the "sea and waves roaring" in that passage, He's not talking about large bodies of water, like the Atlantic Ocean. He's talking about large groups of people—cultural groups, religious groups, language groups, and nationalities—crying out for help from their governments and not getting any! The word "roaring" simply means masses of people in despair, fear, and even panic. They're facing life and death issues, and their governments are unable to solve the problems. It will be the perfect scenario for the anti-Christ to rise to worldwide power.

Second, God has promised to redeem us from every battle we face; that is, He promises to deliver us and give us the victory in every fight of faith, no matter how many battles we're engaged in at any one time. Third, He will deliver us and give us victory through His peace. And finally, that peace will be used to redeem our souls from the battles we fight, not our spirits and not our bodies.

That truth is key! David didn't say God redeemed his spirit or his body from the battles raging all around him. He said the peace of God had redeemed his soul! We are spirits possessing souls and living in bodies. The soul is the mind, will, and emotions—and it's the key component in any fight of faith, because it acts like a spiritual hinge. If our soul is renewed to God and His Word, then our soul will team up with our spirit to control and subdue the flesh. If our soul is unrenewed to the Word of God, it will team up with our dead-to-sin flesh to quench our born-again spirit. Therefore, we must be able to make sound, correct scriptural decisions under pressure—in the midst of, and in the heat of the battle. Peace gives us the ability to do that.

As the day of our Lord's return draws closer, the attacks against the body of Christ are not going to diminish in frequency or intensity. On the contrary, they will be increasing in every way. We need to take advantage of every weapon made available to us by God. One of the most powerful weapons we can use against the devil is the peace of God, yet so few of us understand His peace, take the time to cultivate it, and as a result fail to walk in the light of its power.

I believe God's peace has the inherent power to take us through any attack of the devil, no matter how severe, intense, or prolonged. Like it or not, we are here, and we are in a worldwide fight. Satan will attack the body of Christ collectively and individually. When the attack comes against you, how are you going to respond? How are you going to overcome?

When the battle rages against you, you can stand strong. You can resist the devil. You can be victorious. How? By letting the peace of God redeem you from the attack. Jesus cried over Jerusalem—and Israel in general—because they failed to see and understand the things that made for their peace. (Luke 19:41-44) Now more than ever, we need to avoid making the mistake they made. The battle is not ours, but God's! (2 Chronicles 20:1-30) In these last days I believe this simple truth is vital if we are to hold our position spiritually and advance triumphantly in the name of Jesus.

When Jesus comes back, the Word says He'll be coming back for a triumphant church, without spot or wrinkle. (Ephesians 5:27) That's why 2 Peter 3:14 says, "Therefore, beloved, looking forward to these things, be diligent to be found by Him in peace, without spot and blameless." If we're to be part of this triumphant church, we must be people who know how to walk in God's peace.

Peace is the by-product of faith. When you walk in faith you are walking in true peace. When Jesus comes back, He wants to know if He will find faith on the earth. (Luke 18:8) If you're walking in peace, He'll find you walking in faith!

May God's peace become real to you as you read the truths discussed in this book.

PART I
Legal Peace

CHAPTER 1

Understanding the Necessity, Reality, and Power of Legal Peace

Every year at Christmastime, we see many visual reminders of that blessed and glorious event. Nativity scenes are put up in many public and prominent places. Many retail stores spend much time and money to design and build storefront or aisle displays which depict the birth of our Lord Jesus Christ.

And then we have the Christmas cards! Whether electronically or through the mail, millions of them are sent all over the world to express love, care, and concern between families and friends. Each card tries to visually convey the beauty and majesty of the virgin birth to remind those receiving the card of what Christmas really means to mankind. Beautiful Christmas cards show us an artist's rendition of the nativity scene, the Eastern star that guided the wise men across the deserts, or the angels announcing the Lord's birth to the shepherds tending their sheep on the hillsides outside Bethlehem.

What about those shepherds? The heavenly host assigned by God to announce Jesus' birth to the shepherds had some very interesting things to say about why this miraculous event was taking place.

> *Now there were in the same country shepherds living out in the fields, keeping watch over their flock by night. And behold, an angel of the Lord stood before them, and the glory of the Lord shone around them, and they were greatly afraid.*
>
> *Then the angel said to them, "Do not be afraid, for behold, I bring you good tidings of great joy which will be to all people. For there is born to you this day in the city of David a Savior, who is Christ the Lord. And this will be the sign to you: You will find a Babe wrapped in swaddling clothes, lying in a manger."*
>
> *And suddenly there was with the angel a multitude of the heavenly host praising God and saying: "Glory to God in the highest, and on earth peace, goodwill toward men!"*
>
> —LUKE 2:8-14

What did those angels say? Glory to God in the highest, and on earth peace, goodwill toward men! Peace on earth! The purpose for our Lord's earthly ministry can be summed up in this one basic truth. Jesus came to the earth to establish God's peace on earth with men.

According to Philippians 2:5-11, the second person of the Trinity, Jesus, emptied Himself of all the power and privileges of deity and took upon Himself the form of a lowly human servant. When we look at the virgin birth in this light, we see that this miraculous event was actually an act of love towards man that can never be equaled. God so loved the world He gave Jesus, who came to earth as a man to die in our place and pay the penalty for our sins. Why was all of this done? To establish peace on earth and good-will between God and man.

Jesus Came to Give Back
That Which Was Lost

If Jesus had to come the way He did to establish peace on earth, that means peace on earth had been lost somewhere along the way between God and man. When God created Adam and Eve, this world was one of total peace and tran-quility. The Garden of Eden was perfect in every way—an extension of God's very being and essence.

As God is perfect and the epitome of peace, so was His earth, and the Garden that Adam and Eve were told to take care of. The peace that prevailed on earth at that time was a peace which emanated from the heart and being of God Himself. It was beautiful, perfect, and powerful. It was the environment that God Himself lives in—not because He gives peace, but because He *is* peace! Whenever God creates, His peace is an integral, foundational part of His work.

Adam and Eve had His peace when they were created, but they lost it when they sinned. Thank God He didn't leave us in that condition! He sent Jesus to the earth and then to the cross to pay the price for our sins, which we could never pay ourselves. In doing so, Jesus gave humankind the oppor-tunity to enjoy and live in God's peace once again.

When sin separates us from God, we are separated from His presence. Before sin, God came down in the cool of the day to walk and talk with Adam. But when Adam sinned, that sin made it impossible to enjoy the presence of God and the peace that comes with it. That's why, when the heavenly host sang for the shepherds, they sang about the restoration of peace on earth. They were talking about the peace which Adam lost and the peace which Jesus came to restore. That's one reason why Jesus is referred to as the second Adam. (1 Corinthians 15:45) He came to take back what Satan had stolen from man.

Legal Peace Is Foundational

When we look at the whole canon of Scripture, Genesis to Revelation, we see a big book full of many important things to learn, digest, and understand. The Bible is so rich and so full of spiritual truth, we could easily spend a dozen life-times studying the Word and never even come close to grasping and understanding it all. Even so, there is one foundational truth upon which every other truth is built upon, and that's the necessity of having legal peace with God. Sometimes we get so busy in pursuit of new revelation, we forget this simple yet profound truth. Everything God did in sending Jesus to the earth to be our sin substi-tute was done to restore peace on earth—peace in the heavenlies, and peace in the hearts of men.

When we talk about Christmas and the work Christ came to accomplish, we must remember that everything was done in the light of legal peace. We lost it through Adam, so we needed another Adam to give it back to us. Thank God, His name is Jesus!

.

We Have Legal Peace With God

"Now My soul is troubled, and what shall I say? 'Father, save Me from this hour'? But for this purpose I came to this hour."

—JOHN 12:27

Jesus knew why He had come to earth. He knew He had a purpose. He knew what was going to take place while He hung on the cross. Most of us would say that He allowed Himself to be crucified because He knew we needed a Savior from our sins, and of course, that's true. However, when talking about salvation, it's important to understand what we had and what we lost when Adam sinned. When sin came, man lost the ability to enjoy the presence of God. Man also lost the ability to enjoy the peace that can only come when we are in right standing with God. When man lost his right standing with God legally, he lost the peace that comes with it.

There are two kinds of peace that come from God— legal peace and living peace. When we lost our legal peace with God, we lost our ability to enjoy living peace with God on a daily basis. Legal peace must precede living peace, because legal peace is foundational. We can't enjoy living peace until we've been washed in the blood of the Lamb. *Legal peace deals with our salvation, while living peace deals with our sanctification.* When we accept Jesus as Lord and Savior of our lives, we acquire legal peace with God. From that foundational base, we can then begin to grow and let God's living peace dominate our daily lives. That's why we're looking at legal peace first, because it must precede living peace. Living peace can't be realized in our lives until the issue of legal peace has been settled.

Why? Because the Bible is a legal book. God is a legal God. The Word of God talks about law, and the penalties for breaking that law. It talks extensively about justice and what God demands for justice to be upheld. It describes Jesus as our Advocate, which is a legal term that identifies our Lord as our lawyer. (1 John 2:1)

Jesus sits at the right hand of God, where the Bible says He ever lives to make intercession for us. (Hebrews 7:25)

Legally speaking, that means He's there to represent us and continually plead our case before God. The whole issue of salvation is a legal one. Simply stated, our sin broke God's law. The sentence for breaking God's law is death—spiritual death first, and then eternal death. Spiritual death is a condition—the separation of the human spirit from the Holy Spirit. If a person dies physically in that spiritual condition, without ever having made Jesus the Lord of their life, eternal death follows. They go to hell to spend an eternity separated from the presence and peace of God.

All of this is the way it is because God is a legal and just God. He demands a penalty and payment whenever His law is broken. Romans 11:22 talks about the goodness and the severity of God. His goodness is reflected in the fact that Jesus was sent to the earth to pay the price for our sins. His severity is reflected in the fact that if men refuse His free gift of salvation, they will experience the wrath of God. The sentence for their rebellion will be carried out—no exceptions and no second chances. Hebrews 9:27 says that it's appointed once for man to die, and then comes the judgment. In fact, read the whole book of Hebrews and see what a legal book it is. Hebrews was written to show us that legally we had no hope for salvation, but if we put our trust in what Jesus did for us in obtaining legal peace with God, we can have that free gift of salvation by faith—because our works could never earn it.

When we look closely at the book of Hebrews, we can see exactly what Jesus had to do here on earth. We can see how meticulous He had to be in fulfilling the legal demands of justice. Looking back in the Old Testament we see the same thing in the book of Leviticus. The legal demands for our salvation required a blood sacrifice, not the blood of animals, nor the blood of any ordinary man. It had to be pure human blood—untainted by Adam's sin nature.

Since no man could physically be born of a man and woman with pure, untainted blood, God had to do it Himself. The only way for Him to do that was to become human Himself, which is one of the mysteries of Jesus. He's all God, yet at the same time, He's all man. And how did this come to pass? By virtue of the virgin birth! Because justice demanded pure blood as payment for our sin, Jesus came to the earth, was conceived by the power of the Holy Spirit, and born of a woman.

When we study Isaiah 53, we see a picture of what Jesus had to go through in order to satisfy God's legal demands for justice. Let's look at a portion of what is said in that chapter and see how it pertains to the importance of having legal peace with God.

> *Surely He has borne our griefs and carried our sorrows; yet we esteemed Him stricken, smitten by God, and afflicted.*

> *But He was wounded for our transgressions, He was bruised for our iniquities, the chastisement for our peace was upon Him, and by His stripes we are healed.*

> —ISAIAH 53:4-5

Notice, the chastisement for our peace was upon Him. Through Adam's sin, man lost this peace—a peace which can only come from having right relationship with God. To get that peace back, Jesus was born of a virgin to have the pure blood needed for the remission of our sins. That precious blood was poured out on the cross to pay the penalty God demanded. With our sins laid upon Him on the cross, God's wrath against us was instead poured out upon Jesus. That's why in Isaiah 53:10, the Bible tells us that it pleased God to bruise Jesus as our sin substitute, because in doing so, the penalty we could never pay was paid in full! For the claims of divine justice to be satisfied once for all time, Jesus had to be beaten, battered, bruised, and then murdered on the cross. The shedding of His pure blood was the only way—there was no other option open to Him. In fact, when Jesus was in the Garden of Gethsemene, He pleaded with God for another way to do what needed to be done, but God said no! In His humanity, Jesus recoiled from the thought of going to the cross—and who wouldn't? Crucifixion is one of the most painful ways a man can be put to death. And He wasn't even up there because of something He did, but because of what *we* had done.

> *And He was withdrawn from them about a stone's throw, and He knelt down and prayed, saying, "Father, if it is Your will, take this cup away from Me; nevertheless not My will, but Yours, be done." Then an angel appeared to Him from heaven, strengthening Him.*

> —LUKE 22:41-43

Why did God send an angel to strengthen Jesus? Because He needed it! God was not going to change His mind about His plan for our salvation. Jesus needed to accept that and get on with what God was asking Him to do. The cross was cruel. It was physically painful beyond description. It was humiliating. It was pure torture. And it was all necessary! A legal God demanded it, and His plan had to be carried out. The demands of divine law could not be altered or pacified in any way. There was no "Plan B" for our salvation. It was necessary for Jesus to die like He did to restore peace on earth and goodwill towards men—legal peace between God and man.

On that first Christmas night, when Jesus was born of the virgin Mary, angels were in the heavenlies singing about peace on earth, goodwill towards men. On the cross 33 years later, the chastisement of our peace was upon Him. Our Lord's earthly life and ministry began with a statement of purpose and it ended with the completion of that purpose. His whole life was all about the reacquisition of peace between God and man. It had to be done right and it had to be done legally.

This is why Jesus is the *only* way to salvation (John 14:6). He is not *a* way, but *the* way. To be saved you *must* accept Jesus as Lord and Savior and no other, or you cannot enter the kingdom of God (John 3:3-8). When the Macedonian jailor asked Paul what he *must* do to be saved, he was told to believe on the Lord Jesus Christ, and he would be saved (Acts 16:30-31). That's it, there is no room for debate about it. That's the truth—take it or leave it. Paul didn't tell the jailor there were "many roads leading to heaven." The jailor wasn't told to go and search out the latest philosophy of his day. The jailor wasn't told that Jesus "appears in many forms and in many personalities," depending upon the culture, country, and social strata, so it's okay to worship according to the tenets of the Islamic faith, Buddhist beliefs, Hindu teachings, or any other organized or semi-organized group, religion, idea, or cult that's out there. He was told to accept Jesus—the Jesus of the Bible— period. Why? Because God's justice demanded a pure, sinless sacrifice for our sins, and it was only His Son who could provide, and who did provide, that payment through Calvary's cross. This is a simple message the devil works overtime to complicate.

In today's world of watered-down theology, where preachers and Christians stumble over themselves not to offend anyone in their user-friendly, seeker-friendly (demon-friendly in my opinion) churches, we've got no shortage of lukewarm preachers and teachers coddling their congregants with 20-minute sermonettes full of half-truths, distortions, and lies regarding the true message of salvation. Jesus warned us that just prior to His return to earth, this sort of thing would be happening, and we see it everywhere (Matthew 24:3-5).

Sometime ago I cut out and saved a newspaper clipping from one of the local Tucson, Arizona newspapers. It was from the "religious" section of the paper, where churches advertise themselves to the public. The headline said this: *"We take the Bible seriously but not literally."* After providing the important contact and service information, the ad concluded with, *"Open & Affirming. All are Welcome!"* From time to time, I like to look at that ridiculous statement, just to keep myself motivated to proclaim the full gospel without apology.

On the subject of salvation from sin, it's very politically correct to offer the opinion to people that they can be saved from their sins in any number of ways because it offends nobody, and includes everybody. Everywhere you turn, people are being told salvation is not just through Jesus, or worse, that they can actually live in all kinds of sin with absolutely no intention of changing or repenting—and be perfectly okay with God! With these lies circulating through every possible media outlet these days, there has been a very predictable rise in heresies such as Universalism, with many turning away from the truth because of their "itching ears" (2 Timothy 4:3-4).

The message of love and grace is being grossly distorted by preachers all over the globe, selling thousands of books and filling auditoriums and stadiums with those who love to hear what they want to hear—so they can keep on living any way they want to. We're told a "loving God" could never send people to a place of fire and brimstone to suffer forever, so the definition for hell and for the devil are conveniently changed to accommodate the itching ears of those who turn from the truth to embrace the lie. These imposters and hirelings are disguised as ambassadors of

Christ, pandering to people who want nothing else but to live their lives anyway they want with the sins they love. They search high and low to find themselves preachers, teachers, and churches who claim to be Christian, who tell them it's perfectly okay to go on the way they are because a loving, gracious, merciful God would never be so cruel as to demand a higher, holier, cleaner lifestyle due to His unchanging standards of holiness and purity! Grace is being used as the excuse to live unrepentant lives because after all—God's grace covers us no matter what we do, think, or say. Instead of correctly teaching that God's grace gives us the power to overcome sin, it's being taught as the excuse to continue to live in sin and not be the least bit concerned about it. Once again, all of this was foretold in the Bible, as signs of the end times and of the perilous and difficult times ahead.

Have you noticed this is where we're going as a nation, or have you been living in a cave for the last 30 years? There has always been persecution against Christians because we're righteous people preaching a righteous message in a spiritually dark, dead, and unrighteous world. Jesus Himself told us that when He spoke with Nicodemus on the necessity of receiving Him as the *only* way to obtain salvation (John 3:16-21). But everywhere you turn these days, whether it be on TV, or around the coffee urn at work, or on all the social media outlets like Facebook and Twitter, people love to bash the traditional Christian position on salvation, declaring us to be narrow-minded, bigoted, hate-mongers, religious, exclusive, intolerant, racist, and a host of other descriptions and adjectives too vile and profane to repeat here. They say: "Why do you Christians say that your Jesus is the *only* way? What about the Muslims, Buddhists, devout Catholics, followers of Confucius, new-agers, and millions of others around the world who are all well-meaning seekers of truth and ultimate peace with God? Are you saying none of them are saved, and will never be saved?"

Emphatically, the answer is *yes*! Yes! Yes! Yes! And here's why the answer is yes. Nobody else paid for our sins, that's why! Mohammed didn't pay. Buddha didn't pay. Confucius didn't pay. The Pope or the Virgin Mary didn't pay. Some new-ager with all of his rocks, prisms, beads, and crystals didn't pay. No sir. The *only* one who can be the legal lawyer and mediator between God and man is Christ Jesus. He alone was born of a virgin, shed his pure blood as our sin substitute, went to hell to pay our price, and having been then resurrected from the dead, was declared the son of God with power at the Almighty's right hand in heaven (Romans 1:4), waiting until His enemies are made His footstool (Hebrews 1:13, 10:13). Is that narrow minded? Yes. But is it the truth? Yes again! Didn't Jesus say the road leading to salvation was narrow and difficult (that means He's the only way—no other way), and few (not many, and not everybody) would find it (Matthew 7:14)? Well, if you believe Jesus told the truth, that's it. You either believe that or you don't. There is no alternate way to heaven. There is no other option to consider if you want to go to heaven and not hell when you die—no matter what Hollywood actor, talk show host, or rock star says to the contrary. And therefore, there is no other way to obtain legal peace with God!

God's Peace Replaced His Wrath Towards Us

Because we've been born during the age of God's grace, it's hard for many of us to understand the wrath of God. But if we look in the Old Testament, we see a side of God's nature that, thankfully, we don't have to face today. We're fortunate in that respect.

Because God's complete nature is not fully understood in this age of grace, many of us have a hard time with statements or passages about the wrath of God. In order to fully appreciate the legal peace we enjoy by way of the new birth, we need to appreciate and understand the anger and indignation which wells up inside of God over sin. We have to do this by faith, because Jesus has already reestablished legal peace between God and man.

When we commit sin in this day and age, all we have to do is ask God for forgiveness, be sincere about it, and it's done! Why is that possible? Because all the work was done by Jesus for us. He bore the brunt of God's anger for our sins so we wouldn't have to.

Before Jesus died on the cross and rose from the dead, the people of God had to go through all kinds of religious rituals, just so they could have some kind of communion with God. Why? Because in a legal sense, God was still angry with them for their sins. The penalty had not yet been paid for them. You can see this in reading Psalm 88. In Isaiah 53, the emphasis is upon Jesus as the sacrificial Lamb. But in Psalm 88, the emphasis is upon the wrath of God being poured out on Jesus instead of us.

> *Your wrath lies heavy upon me, And You have afflicted me with all Your waves. I have been afflicted and ready to die from my youth, I suffer Your terrors; I am distraught.*

> *Your fierce wrath has gone over me, Your terrors have cut me off.*

> *They came around me all day long like water; They engulfed me altogether. Loved one and friend You have put far from me, And my acquaintances into darkness.*

> —PSALM 88:7,15-18

What is it we're being shown here? We see the wrath of God being poured out upon Jesus in our place, as our substitute. People living in this dispensation have a hard time seeing God in this light, but this is a part of His nature, just as much as love is a part of His nature. He does get angry, but thank God legal peace has been established between God and man!

It's interesting to note that in the Old Testament, not one time is God ever referred to as the God of peace. Yet when we come over into the New Testament, we see God referred to as the God of peace many times. In the Old Testament we see continuous references to peace offerings being made by the people. But those peace offerings could only cover their sin—they could never remove them. That's why God could not be the God of peace in the Old Testament. Legal peace had not yet been established.

Now that God's anger has been pacified through the work of Calvary's cross, we can come boldly to the throne of God's grace—anytime for anything—to obtain the help we need whenever we need it. (Hebrews 4:16) With Jesus as our heavenly Mediator, legal peace is now a reality between God and man. (1 Timothy 2:4-6) That means we will never have to experience the wrath of God. In fact, 1 Thessalonians 5:9 specifically says that we're not appointed to experience God's wrath, but instead we're to experience His grace.

Thank God for the work of Jesus! If you ever need to be reminded of God's intense hatred and anger over sin, think about the intense pain you would feel if you held your finger for a few seconds over an open flame. Try to imagine untold millions of people feeling that intense pain in hell for all eternity, tormented in the lake which burns with fire and brimstone (Revelation 21:8). (See also Revelation 19:20 and 20:10.) For how long? A few minutes, hours, or days? Just long enough for God to teach them a good lesson they'll never forget? No—for all eternity! If you want to go into mental gridlock, try to imagine being on fire forever—with absolutely no hope for a reprieve or pardon. If that doesn't bring us to our knees in thanksgiving to God, nothing will!

> *Therefore, having been justified by faith, we have peace with God through our Lord Jesus Christ.*

—ROMANS 5:1

When we take the time to study scriptures and see what it means to be on the wrathful side of God's nature, this verse in Romans takes on a whole new element of beauty and preciousness. Because of Jesus, we have peace with God. Present tense legal peace with God! It's not something we're going to get someday when we go to heaven. It's something we have right now. If fact, if we don't have it now in this lifetime, we're not saved! It's that simple.

Legal peace is available—therefore we can be born again. (John 3:3) We can become new creatures in Christ Jesus. (2 Corinthians 5:17) We can become children of God. (John 1:12) We can become partakers of God's divine nature. (2 Peter 1:4) In short, we can now have the kind of relationship with God that He originally intended when Adam and Eve were first created.

> *For He Himself is our peace, who has made both one, and has broken down the middle wall of separation, having abolished in His flesh the enmity, that is, the law of commandments contained in ordinances, so as to create in Himself one new man from the two, thus making peace.*

—EPHESIANS 2:14-15

Here is another New Testament passage talking about legal peace. By dying on the cross as our sin substitute, Jesus became our peacemaker with God. Because Jesus came to earth to be our sin substitute in the eyes of God, all believers—Jews and Gentiles alike—were in Christ when He was hanging on that cross. We were all reconciled to God through Jesus. Jesus is our peace because He and He alone gave us back our legal peace with God.

You see this truth referred to repeatedly throughout the New Testament because it's the very foundation of the Gospel. The very essence of salvation is having legal peace with God.

> *And by Him to reconcile all things to Himself, by Him, whether things on earth or things in heaven, having made peace through the blood of His cross.*

> —COLOSSIANS 1:20

After being raised from the dead, Jesus took His blood into the heavenly Holy of Holies. He placed it upon the mercy seat, at which time the New Testament was put into effect. (Hebrews 9:12) The New Testament legally replaced the Old Testament. It was a legal act to establish a better covenant based upon better promises, establishing legal peace between God and man. That's why Mary couldn't touch Jesus when she encountered Him just outside the burial tomb. (John 20:17) He hadn't yet gone to heaven to put His blood on the mercy seat. But after He did, He came back to the earth and appeared to His disciples. At that time, He encouraged them to handle and touch Him, because the legal work in heaven had already been accomplished. (Luke 24:39) Jesus had made legal peace with God by placing His shed blood on the heavenly mercy seat.

CHAPTER 2

We Are Responsible to Preach Legal Peace

Stand therefore, having girded your waist with truth, having put on the breastplate of righteousness, and having shod your feet with the preparation of the gospel of peace.

—EPHESIANS 6:14-15

As believers, our feet are to be covered with the Gospel of peace. Notice that God specifically calls this Gospel a Gospel of peace, and includes it in the spiritual armor we're told to put on and wear every day. Remember the word "gospel" means good news, and what better news could you share with lost souls?

The penalty for their sins has been paid for, so now nothing stands between them and salvation from God. We're to tell them that they can have peace with God right now—through the finished work of Jesus Christ. They don't have to try to earn heaven, or try to be righteous in the strength of their own works or good intentions. Instead, we're to tell them that Jesus has already made them righteous in Him. The legal work has already been accomplished for them, and for all men everywhere. We can have the joy of telling them that the reality of their own personal salvation is only a faith decision away—an act of their own free will.

What then? Are we better than they? Not at all. For we have previously charged both Jews and Greeks that they are all under sin.

As it is written:

"There is none righteous, no, not one;
There is none who understands;
There is none who seeks after God.
They have all turned aside;
They have together become unprofitable;
There is none who does good, no, not one.
"Their throat is an open tomb,
With their tongues they have practiced deceit";
"The poison of asps is under their lips";
"Whose mouth is full of cursing and bitterness."
"Their feet are swift to shed blood;
Destruction and misery are in their ways;
And the way of peace they have not known."
"There is no fear of God before their eyes."

—ROMANS 3:9-18

When we preach the Gospel, we're to remind people of where we all stood with God before Jesus' death and resurrection. These verses accurately portray man's spiritual condition outside of Christ, but the good news is called good because we get to tell them that all of this was washed away by the blood of Jesus Christ. We couldn't do it for ourselves, so Jesus came and did it for us—that is good news indeed!

When I first got saved and wanted to tell people the good news about Jesus, I bought and distributed gospel tracts. I would peruse the tract catalog from Good News Publishers, based out of Chicago, IL, then pick certain tracts to buy. Once the tracts arrived, I would hand stamp them with the name and address of my local church and pastor, then I would pass them out everywhere I went, as much as I could. I passed them out in bars, airports, airplanes, parking lots (putting them under the windshield wipers of the parked cars), at work, in restrooms every-where, at banks when depositing my paycheck, at restau-rants when ordering my food—anywhere I could. I had tracts in my briefcase, my suit, my topcoat, my gym bag, the glove compartment in my car—everywhere. I averaged 3,000 to 5,000 tracts ordered, stamped, and given out each month for the first year after being born again.

One tract I used was a story-telling picture pamphlet that used illustrations to present the plan of salvation to the reader. One picture in the tract showed God on the left, fallen man on the right, and the word "sin" in the middle between God and man. The illustration was endeavoring to show the reader that sin had separated us from God, thus making it necessary for God to send a Savior to save us from our sins. Even though I completely understand what was being said, and the truth of that illus-tration, from the New Testament perspective that's not an accurate representation for the way things are now.

Yes, in the Old Testament, before Jesus died on the cross and rose from the dead, sin was definitely separating us from a holy and just God. But because Jesus paid for our sins on the cross, the debt was nailed to that cross and our sins were washed away (Colossians 2:13-14). Now, since the resurrection of Christ, sin is no longer between God and man, separating us from Him. However, although sin has been removed and no longer separates us from God, do you know what separates humankind from God now? Jesus! He's the mediator of a better covenant based upon better promises (1 Timothy 2:5, Hebrews 8:6). What separates a man from His God now isn't sin—that was paid for and taken away when Jesus, as the Lamb of God, took away the sin and the sins of the world. Instead, what now separates a person from God is his or her refusal to accept Jesus as Lord as Savior! (John 16:8-11) That's the only sin that keeps a person out of heaven today.

When it comes to the issue of salvation and being born again, the only sin the Holy Spirit convicts a sinner over would be the sin of rejecting the free gift of salvation— making the choice to refuse God's offer to be at peace with Him through Jesus His Son. This is where so many preachers have erred in times past when trying to witness and win souls for Jesus. The gospel is a gospel of peace, not condemnation, not fear, and not a bunch of rules concerning "do's" and "don'ts." Jesus stands at the door to every man's heart and knocks (Revelation 3:20), but we are the ones who have to insert the key and open the door. When you tell people that they can have peace with God by accepting Jesus as Lord and Savior, you're putting that key in their hands and encouraging them to use it to open the door to their heart and invite Jesus in!

Notice again from Romans 3:9-18, that those who reject the free gift of salvation will never know the way of peace. What kind of peace are we talking about here? Legal peace. Those who are evil and choose to stay that way will never know the way of peace. They'll never experience the reality of having legal peace with God. But for anyone who wants it, salvation is a free gift because of Jesus. That is why our Gospel is called the Gospel of peace.

> *"How beautiful are the feet of those who preach the gospel of peace, who bring glad tidings of good things!"*
>
> —Romans 10:15

Our feet are beautiful to God when we preach the Gospel of peace, proclaiming to the world legal peace with God.

We are letting people know they can live free from the bondage of sin by simply accepting their salvation through Jesus Christ by faith. There are no strings attached—no works required—just simple faith in the finished work of Christ. He did all the work to restore God's legal peace to us, and now all we have to do is accept it!

Proclaim Salvation by Proclaiming Peace

How beautiful upon the mountains are the feet of him who brings good news, who proclaims peace, who brings glad tidings of good things, who proclaims salvation, who says to Zion, "Your God reigns!"

—Isaiah 52:7

The message in Romans 10:15 comes from this passage in Isaiah. But notice that here we see the proclamation of salvation coupled with the proclamation of peace. They're together because the entire foundation for salvation is the reacquisition of legal peace with God.

In preaching the Gospel, this must be our foundation. For anyone we meet and are told to witness to by the Holy Spirit, we're to proclaim salvation and peace. This is our job as ambassadors for Christ. (2 Corinthians 5:20) If we represent the Prince of Peace as stated in Isaiah 9:6-7, then we're to present His peace to those who need it.

Let Peace Be God's Magnet

Many Christians get frustrated when their efforts to witness for Christ prove unfruitful. When we don't see results to encourage us, we get discouraged and begin to question our abilities. We tend to feel ill-equipped or inadequate for the task at hand.

Believers who are tempted to feel this way need to let God's peace be the magnet which attracts lost souls to Jesus. After all, we're not the ones responsible for drawing anyone to Jesus. According to John 6:44, God Himself draws sinners to Jesus. John 16:8-11 tells us that He does this through the work of the Holy Spirit. But remember that God works only in partnership with us. He will do the drawing when we do the preaching. And what are we to preach? The Gospel of peace!

This is how we're to cooperate with God in the business of saving souls. We need to work with the Holy Spirit by addressing the real needs in the hearts of those we're witnessing to. You see, we can talk to people all day long about doctrine or the judgment to come, but if we really want to prick their hardened hearts, we should keep addressing the issue of peace in their lives. Why? Because that's what people long for but don't have.

Sinners will sit up and take notice when we start talking to them about an inner peace they can have in Christ. Our Gospel becomes much more effective when we address the innermost longings of the human heart. God made man to live in His peace. Experiencing peace with God then becomes the heart of our message to reach lost humanity.

In these stressed out and pressure-packed times, there is nothing people long for more than inner peace. Peace! People are willing to do almost anything to have it, but they're looking for it in all the wrong places. They try alcohol, illegal drugs, prescription medications, infidelity, sexual perversion, idolatry, job opportunities and career promotions, ad nauseum. A deep inner peace which no one can take from them—that's what people want these days. And that's exactly what the Gospel—and only the Gospel—can give to them, if only we tell them about it.

All we need to do is point them in the right direction and the drawing of the Holy Spirit will take care of the rest. We won't have to convince them to get saved because they'll want to get saved. I believe that's why so many were attracted to Jesus in His earthly ministry. He lived in peace and He was a preacher of peace.

Jesus Was a Preacher of Peace

And He came and preached peace to you who were afar off and to those who were near.

—Ephesians 2:17

The word which God sent to the children of Israel preaching peace through Jesus Christ—He is Lord of all.

—Acts 10:36

When Jesus was born, the heavenly host proclaimed to the shepherds that He had come to bring peace on earth, goodwill towards men. At the close of His earthly life and ministry, as he hung on the cross, the Bible says the chastisement of our peace was upon Him. Now we see from these verses that in between His birth and death, He was called to be a preacher of peace. Can you see how peace was the very foundation for everything He was and everything He did?

Furthermore, Jesus said in John 14:12 that the works He did we should do also. When we think of the works of Jesus, most of us think about His miracles. But His works include the messages He taught and the sermons He preached. In other words, His work included His message as well as His miracles. If He's telling us to do the same works He did, that would include the preaching of peace.

Jesus came to proclaim peace, and that's exactly what we're told to proclaim now in His name. The more we preach and teach about God's peace, the more of an effect it will have on us personally. In my life, I have found that the more I talk about the power of God's peace, the more that peace empowers my life. As I share this truth with others, it brings an increasing element of peace to me. It's a proportionate thing. The more I preach about peace, the more it strengthens me. The less I preach about peace, the less of a stabilizing factor it is in my life.

God's Plan for Our Lives Is Based Upon His Peace

For I know the thoughts that I think toward you, says the Lord, thoughts of peace and not of evil, to give you a future and a hope.

—JEREMIAH 29:11

When God thinks about us, it's in light of the plan He has developed for our lives. Psalm 85:13 says that God will make His footsteps our pathway. That means He's already been where we need to go! He has a plan for our lives and He wants to lead us day by day, step by step. He is where we need to be and wants to take us there according to His perfect plan for our lives. Isn't that comforting to know? God has already gone ahead in our lives to create a pathway that is both blessed and protected.

Notice, when He thinks about the plan He's devised for our lives, His thoughts are always thoughts of peace and not of evil. Why? Because even though God has a different

24

plan for each one of us in the body of Christ, all of His plans have the same foundation. That foundation is peace!

The reason God thinks of us in this way is because His plan for each of us will always have something to do with reaching others in the name of Jesus. Soul-winning is top priority with God, so it will be top priority when He develops His plan for our lives. He's chosen to limit His evangelistic activity on earth to partnership with us.

No matter who we are or where we live, God's plan for our lives will include the preaching of the Gospel of peace to others, either directly or indirectly. No matter who you are today in the body of Christ, God's plan for your life starts and ends with His peace being the dominant force.

Most of us have grossly underestimated the importance of peace in our lives. In the back of our minds we know it's important, but we really haven't taken the time to understand and realize how powerful it is and how strong it can make us. It's important to God, so it must be important to us. We need to be strong if we're to go into all the world to preach this Gospel of peace to the nations.

Once we invite Jesus into our hearts, we're to allow God to develop His plan for our lives as we take the Gospel of legal peace to the world in the name of Jesus. According to God's individual plan for our lives, we're to play our unique part in world evangelism by spreading the Gospel of peace unto the uttermost parts of the earth.

CHAPTER 3

Jesus Put First Things First

In the Bible, there is a principle we've come to call the law of first mention. That simply means that whenever a subject or topic is introduced into scripture for the first time, or when something is said or talked about for the first time, it bears an element of significance. It reveals a spiritual law, principle, or teaching which should play an important role in how we walk out our salvation while living here on earth.

In looking at the ministry of Jesus, it's interesting to see what first came out of His mouth when He first appeared to His disciples, after being raised from the dead. I think it's safe to assume that because time was of the essence, Jesus was not going to be wasting words with His disciples. He was about to go back to heaven and turn everything over to these eleven men. With world evangelism about to begin, and the eternal destinies of multitudes hanging in the balance, you can be sure that Jesus was not going to waste any time getting to the important things He needed to discuss. He was going to get right to the major issues. He was going to teach, review, and reassure them concerning the most basic, fundamental truths they were responsible to know and share in the years to come.

Jesus knew how severe the persecution and demonic attacks would be against them once they launched out to obey His command in Mark 16:15-18. He knew what they were going to need to stay faithful and not compromise, draw back, or fall away. We can be sure Jesus was not going to spend time talking about unnecessary things that wouldn't be foundational to their spiritual stability and success.

Now as they said these things, Jesus Himself stood in the midst of them, and said to them, "Peace to you."

—Luke 24:36

Then, the same day at evening, being the first day of the week, when the doors were shut where the disciples were assembled, for fear of the Jews, Jesus came and stood in the midst, and said to them, "Peace be with you."

When He had said this, He showed them His hands and His side. Then the disciples were glad when they saw the Lord.

So Jesus said to them again, "Peace to you! As the Father has sent Me, I also send you."

—John 20:19-21

And after eight days His disciples were again inside, and Thomas with them. Jesus came, the doors being shut, and stood in the midst, and said, "Peace to you!"

—John 20:26

There are many things Jesus could have talked about when He appeared to His men after being raised from the dead. All of them would have been important in and of themselves. He could have talked about righteousness, joy, love, authority, faith, judgment, forgiveness of sins, or any number of other important New Testament topics.

But look at what He talked about first. It was the peace of God! When appearing to His closest men for the first time after His resurrection, the first words out of His mouth dealt directly with the peace of God. Why? Because it's the foundation for everything Jesus came to accomplish for God and man. It's why He came to the earth in the first place—to be our sin substitute and get back the legal peace we lost through Adam's sin.

When Jesus greeted His disciples, He greeted them by saying, "Peace be unto you." (Luke 24:36 KJV) There were two things He was saying in that statement. First, He's telling all of us that legal peace has now been made a reality between God and man. Sin is no longer standing between God and man anymore—He has taken it out of the way. God is not angry with man anymore. The price for our sins has been paid and the claims of divine justice satisfied. This all deals with the legal aspect of God's peace.

Second, He's telling all of us that when we are born again, we not only enjoy the reality of having legal peace with God, but can now enjoy the blessings of a living peace each and every day. As we go into all the world as ambassadors for Christ, living peace will give us the strength to stand firm when intense persecution comes against us.

In one simple statement, Jesus was telling us we have legal peace with God, and because of that we can now experience the power of living peace on a daily basis.

Evangelism and God's Peace Must Go Together

In John 20, verses 19, 21, and 26, Jesus spoke "peace" three times, twice when Thomas was not there and once when he was. When Jesus said this the second time, He said He was sending us into the world as God had sent Him into the world. Actually, He was reminding them of what He had already prayed back in John 17. He had prayed and interceded for them just before His arrest and crucifixion.

As You sent Me into the world, I also have sent them into the world.

—JOHN 17:18

We see that Jesus combined our need for peace with our responsibility to evangelize the world. He's showing us that in order to go into all the world to win souls effectively, we've got to go in the peace of God. We must allow God's peace to rule and reign in our lives daily if we are to accurately present the Gospel of peace! Doesn't that make sense? After all, how can we accurately represent the Prince of Peace with the Gospel of peace if we're not living and walking in peace? It's a bit hypocritical, don't you think?

Going back to all that Jesus could have talked about when He first appeared to His disciples in the upper room, realize that the only two topics He addressed in that whole exchange were God's peace and world evangelism. Can you see the significance of that?

Having legal peace and walking in living peace are directly tied to effective world evangelism. We can't preach legal peace to others if we've not yet experienced it ourselves. And we can't preach effectively to others about legal peace if we're not walking in living peace personally on a daily basis.

Through salvation we obtain the reality of God's legal peace in our hearts and lives. At that point our relationship with God begins to develop and we learn how to walk in the light of His living peace on a daily basis. Through the indwelling presence of the Holy Spirit, the peace of God begins to dominate our walking, talking, and thinking.

More and more, His peace rules and dominates every area of our daily lives.

Eight days after our Lord's initial appearing, Thomas was with the others who had seen and talked to Jesus earlier. When Jesus appeared the second time, again, the first thing out of His mouth was a salutation of peace. In His first appearance, He spoke "peace" twice. When He appeared when Thomas was with them eight days later, He said it again. It wasn't the last thing He mentioned before He disappeared, or something which was inserted into a running discussion with His disciples. It was the first thing He talked about in both of these incidents.

If Jesus thinks it's this important, it needs to be that important for us! Legal peace and living peace: We can't have relationship with God without legal peace, and we can't effectively represent Jesus to the world evangelistically without living peace. We need them both, and thank God both are available!

PART II
Living Peace

CHAPTER 4

Walking in the Light of Legal Peace

*For unto us a Child is born, unto us a Son is given;
and the government will be upon His shoulder. And His
name will be called Wonderful, Counselor, Mighty God,
Everlasting Father, Prince of Peace.*

—Isaiah 9:6

Jesus Is Peace Himself

Jesus is called the Prince of Peace. He doesn't just possess peace, He *is* peace! When He becomes Lord and Savior of our lives, we not only experience the legal peace made available through His death and resurrection, but we gain the ability to walk in His peace daily. You see, it's one thing to have legal peace with God, but quite another to walk in the light of who He is every day.

A person can be born again, on their way to heaven, and still be unable to cast all their daily cares upon the Lord. They may enjoy legal peace with God, but their personal life is in shambles.

In my ministry travels around the world, I've encountered many believers who have legal peace with God but fail to walk in the power of that peace daily. They enjoy the legal part of God's total peace package, but fail to enjoy the living part. Although they're saved and assured of an eternity with God, they lack what it takes to live a victorious life daily. Victory over fear. Victory over worry. Victory over demonic oppression. Victory over the opinions of others. Victory over a bad medical report. Victory over any situation!

In my own Christian life, as I work out my salvation (Philippians 2:12) in service to the Lord, I've also been guilty of surrendering my living peace on many occasions. By experience, I know how quickly and easily Christians can lose that living peace if we're not vigilant to protect it daily.

Not walking in living peace is very common with believers, and it's time to change! As it says in Psalm 55:18, we need the peace of God every day—otherwise we're not going to have the strength to stand against Satan in these last days of spiritual battle.

> *Evening and morning and at noon I will pray, and cry aloud, and He shall hear my voice. He has redeemed my soul in peace from the battle that was against me, for there were many against me.*

—PSALM 55:17-18

One of the reasons David was called a "man after God's own heart" (Acts 13:22) is illustrated right here, in these two verses. He was a man of great prayer, and specifically, a man who didn't just know the importance of prayer, but also the faith that must be exhibited when praying. Notice he prayed evening, morning, and at noontime, and that when he did, he was "crying out to the Lord," declaring the end result by faith. So many of us know how to "cry aloud" to the Lord alright, but only in fear, doubt, and unbelief! That's how many Christians cry out to the Lord in prayer, but that's not how David did it. When he prayed, he prayed often and with purpose. He laid his case out before the Lord, trusted Him for the answer, and then declared it with the words of his mouth. His prayers were faith prayers indeed.

But also notice the reasons for why he was praying three times a day. Verse 18 tells us that David was in prayer because of the many battles that were against him. Not just one or a few, but many! Have you ever been attacked simultaneously by the devil on several fronts at the same time? I have, many times. This is not by accident. Satan works hard to organize and camouflage, and then launches as many attacks as he can against us at the same time—with the hope of overwhelming us and forcing us to cave in and depart from the faith.

In professional American football, there is a penalty called "piling on." It's a 15-yard penalty against the defense for piling on top of the ball carrier after he has been tackled and the play whistled dead by the referees. Once the play is declared over by the officials, the ball carrier must be allowed to get up off the ground, but if the defensive players refuse to let him up, and begin to "pile on top" of the guy still on the ground, that's a 15-yard penalty assessed against the defense.

Have you ever felt like the devil was "piling on" when dealing with his attacks against you? He doesn't just attack your finances, but your marriage, your family, your job, your health, and your dog—all at the same time! It's not just one thing, but many things coming against you! Just when you think things can't or won't get any worse—they do! This is what David was experiencing in Psalm 55:17-18. He was being attacked on many fronts simultaneously. Notice he talks not just about one battle, but many battles against him.

In the midst of these simultaneous attacks and battles, David declares in faith that His God would redeem his soul in peace from the battles coming against him. He believes in his God. He has faith that God will come through. He believes it with his heart, and confesses it with his mouth. That's the way of faith, according to the New Testament (Romans 10:9-10). What we believe in our heart is spoken out of our mouths! It's called the "spirit of faith" in 2 Corinthians 4:13.

But there's something else to take note of here. David doesn't say God will redeem his spirit or his body from the battles raging against him. He says God will redeem his soul from those battles. In every battle you will ever fight the fight of faith with, your soul will be the key to victory or defeat. Not the spirit and not the body—but the soul. Why? Because the soul consists of the mind, will, and emotions. It's where you do your thinking, decision-making, and planning. It's where you express yourself in your "there's-nobody-like-me-because-I'm-a-unique-one-of-a-kind-creation-by-the-hand-of-God" way. It's the hinge in our tri-partite nature.

We are spirits possessing souls and living in bodies. Majority will always rule on the issue of spirituality verses carnality. If the soul is renewed to·the Word of God, then the renewed soul will team up with the born-again spirit, and dominate and control the dead-to-sin flesh. On the other hand, if the soul is unrenewed to the Word of God, it will team up with the dead-to-sin flesh, and dominate and control the born-again spirit. Two against one always wins—always!

David knew what we need to know today. God's peace will redeem (save, renew, and protect) our souls in times of spiritual, emotional, or fleshly attack.

As I've said, I know in my own life and ministry, there have been too many times when I've allowed the lies of the enemy; the people he influences, uses, or controls; and the situations he creates to steal my peace. I've never lost my legal peace with God, but I've let the devil rob me of living peace—the peace I need to function effectively here on earth for Jesus. I never stopped being saved, but I lost the peace I needed to overcome the challenge of the devil for that moment in my life. In essence, I lost my living peace while continuing to enjoy legal peace with God. Most of us have let this happen more times than we'd like to count!

To enjoy life to its fullest, Christians need to be people of peace. To be as effective as possible in leading sinners to Christ, believers need to be people of peace. In Proverbs 12:20, we're told that *counselors of peace will have joy!* The more we allow God's peace to dominate our lives daily, the better we'll be at presenting the gospel of peace to the unbelievers, because our spiritual counsel to them (what we call witnessing) will be so full of peace and joy, those we're witnessing to will *want* what they see we have!

We should not be people who only enjoy our legal peace with God, but fail to live out the reality of that peace on a daily basis. Thank God for the legal peace that only the born-again experience can bring, but we also need the power to live our lives victoriously—not just once in a while, but consistently, day after day. In good times and bad, our lives must be testimonies to the indwelling presence of the Holy Spirit. According to Isaiah 54:13, *great shall be the peace of our children!* That means our living peace isn't just for Sunday at church, but at home with our spouse and children, at work with our co-workers, on location whenever and wherever we travel, and in every other area of our day-to-day routine. God's living peace, manifested in our lives, becomes one of the most powerful magnets we are ever going to have in attracting lost people to Jesus.

Thank God for legal peace, but let's not stop there, because God did not stop there. Jesus died and rose from the dead to provide legal peace and living peace. Let's enjoy the benefits of both! Let us always be thankful for our salvation, but let's go on and allow the power of who Jesus is to become a daily wall of protection against Satan. Let's allow the Prince of Peace to have free reign in our lives, to rule and dominate our words, thoughts, and actions.

Every day we need to let the power of God's peace protect us from the attacks we face from Satan. At the same time, we are to allow God's living peace to be the magnet that draws the sinner to the Jesus they see in us. It opens a door of utterance we can take advantage of, and as a result, lead many into the born-again experience. It's a win-win situation! We walk in the joy of living peace daily, and at the same time become a true "walking witness" for the Lord Jesus Christ. We're blessed, and sinners are brought into the family of God. The only loser in all of this is the devil!

Jesus Is the King of Peace

For this Melchizedek, king of Salem, priest of the Most High God, who met Abraham returning from the slaughter of the kings and blessed him, to whom also Abraham gave a tenth part of all, first being translated "king of righteousness," and then also king of Salem, meaning "king of peace," without father, without mother, without genealogy, having neither beginning of days nor end of life, but made like the Son of God, remains a priest continually.

—HEBREWS 7:1-3

I believe this passage is a prophetic reference to our Lord Jesus Christ. I'm aware that there is debate in the Christian community about who this Melchizedek really was, but for me the debate is over. I believe the Word of God clearly explains itself and shows us that Melchizedek was in fact an Old Testament appearance of the Lord Jesus Himself

Who else on the earth—besides Adam and Eve—was without father or mother? Who else was without a genealogy or family history? Who else but Jesus had neither beginning of days nor end of life, when looking at eternity past and eternity future? With all of this being said to describe this man Melchizedek, who else could realistically be called one "who is made like unto the Son of God"? And finally, who else but Jesus could be called king of Salem, or king of peace? To me, only one man could fit this description, and His name is Jesus.

He came to Abraham in the person of Melchizedek and received a tenth of the spoils. This was done not just to teach us the principle of tithing, but to show us who Jesus is. In the Old Testament as well as in the New Testament, His nature does not change. Jesus is both the Prince of Peace and the King of Peace. He is our peace and He has broken down all the legal walls separating us from God. In doing that, He has made God's living peace available for us to enjoy every day. It's this living peace which guards our hearts and minds, enabling us to reign in life as kings and priests which is what God intended for man all along.

Jesus Left Us His Peace

Peace I leave with you, My peace I give to you, not as the world gives do I give to you. Let not your heart be troubled, neither let it be afraid.

—JOHN 14:27

If Jesus left us His peace, He obviously intended for us to take advantage of its power. He wants us to experience His peace daily, and let it be the powerful force we need to stay strong in the Lord.

We're told not to let our hearts be troubled, or let our hearts be afraid. That means we have a choice, which means it's our responsibility. It's not up to God or the devil—it's up to us. We don't have to be fearful or troubled. We can choose to rise above the enemy's temptation and walk upon the high places of the earth. (Isaiah 58:14) We can choose to cast down every imagination which exalts itself against the knowledge of God and walk in the peace of God instead. (2 Corinthians 10:3-5) We can choose to walk in fear or walk in faith. We can choose to walk in stress or walk in peace. The choice is ours to make, and nobody else can make these choices in our lives except us!

How are we to rise above the fear, stress, and anxiety which permeates our society? With so many people overcome by the pressures of day-to-day living and slaves to the social disease of stress, how are we to separate ourselves effectively? How can we successfully and consistently guard our hearts from fear? The answer is very simple.

> Then the Lord said to him, "Peace be with you, do not fear, you shall not die." So Gideon built an altar there to the Lord, and called it The-Lord-Is-Peace.

> —JUDGES 6:23-24

According to this passage, *God's peace is His antidote for fear.* When we let our hearts follow after God's peace, we can effectively quench every fiery dart Satan tries to implant in our minds. We can be free from fear, or we can choose to live under its bondage. We're free moral agents. We have the God-given power to choose.

Remember, in a legal sense God is never referred to in the Old Testament as the God of Peace. Why, then, did Gideon name his altar The-Lord-Is-Peace? Because in this passage we're talking about living peace, not legal peace. If you read chapters six and seven of Judges carefully, you can see that Gideon had a face-to-face encounter with the Lord Jesus Christ, who in this story is called the Angel of the Lord. (Judges 6:22) It's much like what Abraham experienced when he met Jesus as Melchizedek, who was described as the King of Peace.

Gideon was called a mighty man of valor (Judges 6:12) and told to deliver God's people from the oppression of the enemy. As the angel of the Lord, Jesus appeared to Gideon to empower him and help him overcome the temptation to fear. Through the indwelling presence of the Holy Spirit, isn't that exactly what He wants to do in our lives today?

The manifestation of our Lord's living peace is not for when we get to heaven, but for now, in this life and in these last days. In John 14:27 Jesus said that His peace had been given—past tense. That means it's for now—in this time and in this life. Why? Because now more than ever we need an effective antidote for fear!

> *And there will be signs in the sun, in the moon, and in the stars; and on the earth distress of nations, with perplexity, the sea and the waves roaring; men's hearts failing them from fear and the expectation of those things which are coming on the earth, for the powers of the heavens will be shaken.*

> —Luke 21:25-26

When talking about the signs to indicate the end of this age, Jesus specifically said that one such sign would be the prevalence of fear throughout the earth. For the unbelievers we can understand that, but what about the children of God? Are we supposed to fall prey to the prevailing force of fear in these last days? Decidedly not! We're supposed to be different. We're called to live in peace and preach the Gospel of peace throughout the earth—especially in these last days!

We're not supposed to be like those who don't know Jesus as Lord and Savior. We're not supposed to live under the bondage of fear like they do. We're called to be divine magnets, attracting the lost to God. It will happen when they see the power of God's living peace in our lives. When they see us walking above fear in the peace of God, they'll want what we have!

Every child of God has the Holy Spirit dwelling in their heart. By virtue of His presence in their heart, they have the ability to live above the fears which control the lives of untold millions on the earth today. First John 4:4 says, "Greater is the Holy Spirit in us than our enemies living in the world" (my paraphrase). Do we let that truth dominate our daily lives? Is that truth allowed to create a fortress of peace each day? In most cases, sad to say, the answer is no.

We've been born again to be different—to be separated. We're a chosen generation, a royal priesthood, and a holy nation. (1 Peter 2:9) We're called God's own special people, proclaiming God's praises in thanksgiving for calling us out of darkness and into His marvelous light.

In John 14:27, Jesus said that the peace He's leaving with us does not come from the world. It's from Him and Him alone. No one on earth, no matter how well-intentioned they may be, can give us this kind of peace—not our doctor, lawyer, or banker; not our analyst, psychologist, or psychiatrist; not even our pastor or our spouse if we're married. We can't find this peace in our mutual funds, the stock market, or in any other kind of financial investment.

Our bank accounts can be full of money, but that won't give us the kind of peace that Jesus offers.

The entire world is looking and searching for this inner peace, but they're looking in all the wrong places! They won't find this peace in alcohol, drugs, infidelity, financial success, the accumulation of wealth and all that it can buy, career success, or educational accomplishments, such as degrees, diplomas, and fancy titles with many initials! *They'll never find it unless they open their hearts and let Jesus become the Lord of their lives!* They can search their entire life, and will never find the kind of peace that they know is out there, and the kind of peace they want desperately—until Jesus becomes their Lord and Savior. That's it.

The only place we're going to find this kind of peace is with the Lord. It's really sad to see people looking all over the place to find that which only Jesus can offer. Peace! Peace of mind and peace of heart. Legal peace and living peace. It can't be found in drugs or alcohol. It can't be found in the eastern religions or New Age thinking. It can only be found when we surrender our hearts and minds to the Lord.

> *These things I have spoken to you, that in Me you may have peace. In the world you will have tribulation; but be of good cheer, I have overcome the world.*
>
> —JOHN 16:33

What a comforting statement! In Jesus, we have peace! Legal peace and then, hopefully, living peace. Legal peace comes when we make Jesus the Lord of our lives. Living peace comes when we make Jesus Lord every day of our lives. Understand that there is a big difference between the two!

In the world, we will have tribulation. We will be attacked. We will suffer persecution. We will be tried and tested. We will have opportunity to cave in to pressure and stress. Jesus said so. This is not a "maybe," but just as certain as you are sitting there reading this book right now. However, notice that even though Jesus said we will come under attack, how we respond is completely up to us. We can hang our heads and shuffle through life in a state of continuous depression, or we can lift our heads up high, take a deep breath, and let the power of God's peace deliver us. How often? As often as the attacks come!

Many are the afflictions of the righteous, but the Lord delivers him out of them all.

—PSALM 34:19

Proverbs 24:10 says that if we quit in the day of adversity, our level of strength is very low. In other words, if we give up in the middle of our fight of faith, we're very weak spiritually. Is that what we're supposed to be like in these last days? Are we to give up and yield to the pressures to conform to this world? Are we to throw up our hands and accept defeat? Are we to become slaves to sleeping pills, ulcer remedies, prescription drugs, and the analyst's counseling recommendations? No! No! No!

Even though we will be tested and experience many difficulties along life's way, Jesus didn't say we should resign ourselves to perpetual depression and despair. He said to be of good cheer! That means we should let the joy of the Lord be our strength. (Nehemiah 8:10) We're to put a smile on our faces and let the world know we have peace from the inside out. Believe me, it will do wonders for you and for multitudes around you. Our peace will not only be a blessing to us, but affect all those around us in a positive way. Isn't that what it means to be the salt of the earth and the light of the world? (Matthew 5:13-14)

Jesus Has Already Overcome Our Enemies

Why be of good cheer? Why be joyful? Because Jesus said He has already overcome the world. That's past tense once again. The Bible teaches that we have three enemies we must face and overcome in this life. The first would be the devil and all the demons who work for him. The second would be the world system, of which Satan is god. The third would be our flesh.

Now here's the good news. Jesus overcame the devil and all his demons. (Hebrews 2:14) Jesus overcame the world system. (John 14:27, 2 Corinthians 4:4, Romans 6 and 7) Lastly, Jesus overcame the power of sin in our flesh. (Hebrews 2:14-18; 10:5) Praise God—Jesus beat them all and handed us His victory! What more do we need to establish the foundation of peace in our hearts and minds?

Our enemies are defeated! It is done and there is nothing they can do about it. They can huff and puff, but they can never blow our house down unless we let them. Satan has no legal power over us anymore. We can walk free from sin and compromise by simply allowing God's living peace to gain ascendancy in our thoughts, words, and actions.

> And let the peace of God rule in your hearts, to which also you were called in one body; and be thankful.
>
> —COLOSSIANS 3:15

This sounds exactly like what Jesus said in John 14:27. Don't let your heart be troubled or afraid. Let God's peace rule over the situation, no matter how impossible things might look in the natural. In order to do that, we have to focus our attention upon the condition of our hearts—not the physical organ that pumps blood through our bodies, but our spirit man living on the inside.

Peace is a spiritual force that resides within the spirit of man. It's not a feeling, but when allowed to dominate, it will produce the right kinds of feelings. It fills our heart with a power no demon or demon-controlled man can touch.

The living peace of God has the power to take us to a place where we can actually become independent of the circumstances around us. It can happen, but it requires our time and attention. It's not automatic because it still demands us to make the right choice. We have to decide not to accept things the way the devil wants them to be in our lives. Instead, we have to decide to live in the protection and provision of God's living peace.

Living peace is available. The world can't give it to us, and the world can't take it away from us. Don't be satisfied with having only legal peace with God. Thank God for that, but learn to move on. So many are saved, but helpless to stand against the demonic onslaught being brought against them in these last days. So many are on their way to heaven, but useless to God while living here on earth. We must not let that happen to us!

If we don't build upon the foundation of God's legal peace, we'll be neutralized by our enemies. In essence, we'll just be taking up time and space here on earth and doing nothing to impact people's lives for Jesus. We'll be just like nonbelievers in the world.

It's the living peace of God, flowing through us and dominating our lives in every way, that makes us different from everyone else. Are we better than they in the eyes of God? Of course not! God is not a respecter of persons. (Acts 10:34) It's just that we have decided to tap into a power source they know nothing about. It's available to anyone, just like it was available to us, but others have to make the right choices like we do. Anyone can have this peace. All they have to do is use their faith to get saved and decide to accept nothing less than total peace on a daily basis—just like we have to do.

That's the good news which attracts people to the Lord Jesus Christ through us. They see we have a peace they want but don't know how to get, which gives God an open door into their heart. They know that anyone can go to the doctor or the bank to get help, but when they understand that Christians are the only ones who can have this kind of inner peace from the Lord, they'll be wanting us to tell them all about Jesus! When they see the power of peace manifested in our lives daily, they'll want it for themselves—especially when they realize it's free—no doctor bills, hospital bills, drug bills, or counseling fees. The longer they look at it, the more attractive it becomes.

CHAPTER 5

Living Peace Guards Our Hearts and Minds

And the peace of God, which surpasses all under-standing, will guard your hearts and minds through Christ Jesus.

—PHILIPPIANS 4:7

The living peace of God goes beyond all earthly under-standing. Unsaved people can't identify it, isolate it, or analyze it. They can't label it, study it, or control it. They can only acknowledge its power in the lives of those who have enough sense to yield to it. God's peace can guard our hearts and minds like nothing else can.

Live above the Attack through Peace

It's sad to see so many Christians living their lives as slaves to their circumstances. They're recipients of God's legal peace, blood-bought, and on their way to heaven yet at the same time, slaves to the external forces around them. So many believers are captive to their feelings, emotions, outside social opinion, or demonic oppression and attack.

Thank God they're saved, but they're totally useless for the kingdom of God. Satan has successfully made them of no effect for the work of world evangelism. The power of his demonic fear has usurped the place that God's peace was designed to hold. In short, they have hearts and minds which are unprotected, and the devil will take full advantage of that.

Let's not be like that in the body of Christ! Let's be pleasing to the Lord. Let's walk by faith and let God's peace govern us at all times, everywhere. In this day and age, only the peace of God has the ability to guard our hearts and minds. There is simply no other way—and frankly, there doesn't need to be any other way. God's living peace is more than enough.

> *He has delivered us from the power of darkness and conveyed us into the kingdom of the Son of His love, in whom we have redemption through His blood, the forgiveness of sins.*

—COLOSSIANS 1:13-14

We have redemption through our Lord's shed blood. We have received forgiveness of sins. These truths speak of the legal peace we have by virtue of the new birth. However, being delivered from the power of darkness is a legal reality that needs to be lived in daily. To make this truth a legal reality in our lives, we need only accept Jesus as Lord and Savior. But from that point on, we can look at these verses in a different light—the light of living peace.

If we've been taken out of the devil's kingdom through the work of Jesus, and if we've received our salvation by faith in our Lord's work, we need to enjoy the fruits of the work daily. We can't change the past, but we can do something about our future. If we've let the devil steal our living peace, let's not waste time feeling sorry for ourselves.

According to Philippians 3:13, let's forget the things behind us, and move on to what lies ahead. If we've failed to walk in the light of God's living peace, let's not wallow in self-pity. Let's get up and grow. With the help of the Holy Spirit, make a more concerted effort to let God's peace rule and reign in your life. The more we attend to this issue in our lives, the better our batting average will be.

Peace Should Be Increasing in Our Lives

For unto us a Child is born, unto us a Son is given; and the government will be upon His shoulder. And His name will be called Wonderful, Counselor, Mighty God, Everlasting Father, Prince of Peace. Of the increase of His government and peace there will be no end.

—ISAIAH 9:6-7

When we looked at this verse earlier, we focused on the fact that Jesus is called the Prince of Peace. Now we see that His government and His peace should be increasing as time goes by. That means the living peace of God is supposed to be growing and developing in us. It's supposed to become more dominant in our lives as time goes by. It's a growing and maturing process—God's peace ruling and reigning to a greater and greater degree in our lives. Peter understood this truth and used it to greet those he wrote to.

Grace to you and peace be multiplied.

—1 PETER 1:2

Grace and peace be multiplied to you in the knowledge of God and of Jesus our Lord.

—2 PETER 1:2

In both of his inspired letters, Peter talks about the multi-plication of peace. We know he can't be talking about legal peace, because that's a one-time acquisition. A person is either born again or not born again. We can't be at differ-ent levels or stages of being born again. We are either saved or unsaved—it's one or the other. So these statements can't be referring to legal peace.

As Isaiah looks ahead prophetically concerning the life, ministry, and kingdom of Jesus, Peter is talking about the development of living peace in a believer's life. When Jesus left us His peace, He intended for it to grow and be cultivated with the help of the Holy Spirit. As a spiritual force within us, the living peace of God has the inherent ability to grow. If we are growing in grace the way we should be, the level of peace we walk in today should be more than what it was in our lives one year ago. The more time we spend with God in prayer and in His Word, the more His peace will dominate our thoughts, words, and actions. It doesn't happen overnight, but it will happen if we're diligent to apply ourselves to the task. God's living peace is designed to increase in our lives as we grow and mature in Christ.

Notice that Peter said the peace of God will multiply in knowledge. That means that the more we know of God, the more potential there is for God's living peace to take control of our lives. Notice I said potential. It still boils down to the choices each of us must make. Even when we learn and know more about God, we still must decide to act upon that newfound knowledge. We still must not let our hearts be troubled or become afraid.

Jesus knew God better and more intimately than any other human being. That's why He was so supernatural and at peace at the same time. You've got to have peace about who God is to cruise across the lake on foot, to multiply a few pieces of bread and fish twice to feed thousands, or to raise dead bodies and call them out of tombs. You've got to have peace about who God is to let ungodly, religious liars arrest you, condemn you unjustly, and nail you to a cross.

How could Jesus do such things with such confidence and strength? Because he walked in such peace with God. Nothing could frighten Him or shake Him. In Mark 4:37-38, it says He was fast asleep in the middle of the lake during a raging windstorm. His disciples were terrified for their lives, but He was at such peace with God. He was so sound asleep that they had to come and shake Him to wake Him! How could Jesus be this way? Through the knowledge of His Father God.

Just like Jesus, we can grow and multiply in peace as we learn more and more about God. Romans 15:33 calls God a God of peace. It stands to reason that the more time we spend with Him, the more His peace will affect our lives. In fact, all through the New Testament, God is repeatedly referred to as the God of peace. It's quite a different picture than the God we see portrayed in the Old Testament. In addition to Romans 15:33, you'll find God is called the God of peace in Romans 16:20, Philippians 4:9, 1 Thessalonians 5:23, and Hebrews 13:20.

In the Old Testament, God was predominantly portrayed as the God of anger, indignation, and wrath. He was the God who demanded strict adherence to the Mosaic Law, as given in the first five books of the Old Testament. Because legal peace had not yet been secured through Christ, living peace was out of the question.

Now that's not to say that everybody in the Old Testament was depressed, gloomy, and melancholy all day long. They had joy and thanked God when it dominated their lives. But the peace we can enjoy now is not something they could tap into, simply because the Holy Spirit wasn't yet living in their hearts. Nobody was born again. So how much more should we be doing for God? We have no excuses for failure. We have the power of God's living peace at our disposal.

We're Called to Peace

And let the peace of God rule in your hearts, to which also you were called in one body, and be thankful.

—COLOSSIANS 3:15

In one body, we were all called to peace. To let living peace rule and reign daily is our God-given call in this life. It's part of God's perfect will for all believers.

But if the unbeliever departs, let him depart; a brother or a sister is not under bondage in such cases. But God has called us to peace.

—1 CORINTHIANS 7:15

In context, this passage is talking about marital relationships. Although we understand that, God reveals a spiritual truth that transcends the context. It's the same message from Colossians 3:15. We're called to peace—not just in marriage, but in everything. The marriage relationship was designed by God to be a relationship rooted and grounded in love, and the peace that comes from love. But God's living peace goes far beyond that. It's designed to encompass every aspect of human existence and give us the ability to be overcomers. No matter what, we're to live in God's peace and be more than conquerors through Christ, who loved us and gave Himself for us. (Romans 8:37)

If we're made in the image and likeness of God, we're going to be people of peace. Jesus was a mirrored reflection of God. (John 14:9) We're supposed to be mirrored reflections of Jesus. (Romans 8:29) Jesus walked in such peace because He knew His Father God, and He knew They were one. We are to walk in peace because we know Jesus, and we know that we are one with Him. (1 Corinthians 6:17)

When God created Adam, His intent was to create man as a mirrored reflection of His essence and glory. Psalm 8:5 says that man was made a little lower than the Godhead. That means that when man was created, he was created with such brilliance and intelligence, he was just below God Himself! So the reason we're called to peace is because we're called to be just like God, and peace is a part of God's very being.

Wherever Jesus went, He influenced people with His power and peace. We need to be so much like Him that we do the same thing when we meet people every day. When Jesus came on the scene, His very presence was a stabilizing factor. He really didn't even have to say anything—just His presence exuded the power and peace of God. Just by walking into a situation, people knew this Man was full of power and peace.

Are we like that today? Sadly, not many of us are. Does our very presence bring a stabilizing force in the midst of chaos, anxiety, fear, and confusion? Do people just "relax" when they know we've arrived? Or are we something less than that? Are we nothing more than a bunch of "Brother Blend-ins"? You know who Brother Blend-in is, don't you? That's the Christian who thinks like the world, talks like the world, and acts like the world. He's good friends with "Pastor Popular." The two of them constitute the vast majority of people who call themselves children of God.

Separate yourself! Let God's peace sanctify you, and set you apart from the rest of the pack. The more you allow

God's living peace to guide you, the more sanctified you will become.

God's Peace Will Lead Us

For you shall go out with joy, and be led out with peace.

—ISAIAH 55:12

What is supposed to lead us? The peace of God. It's to lead and guide us each day with the affairs of life. That's why God's Word encourages us to seek the Lord early each day. When we have finished our early time of communion with God, we've surrounded ourselves with the peace needed to manage the rest of the day in the strength of our spirit, not in the weakness of our dead-to-sin flesh.

At work, at school, or at play—is God's peace guiding you and leading you forth? For most believers it is not. And even though I have many times been guilty of failing to follow God's peace throughout my day, I'm purposing in my heart to change. I want to follow God's peace because I know it will guard me and never lead me astray. You need to make the same decision too.

The days ahead are not going to be pleasant. As the return of Jesus draws closer, the Word of God clearly indicates a time of unparalleled chaos, confusion, and fear (see Matthew 24 and Luke 21). If you think things have been bad up to this point in time, I have news for you. It's going to get worse! This world as we know it is heading towards a meltdown the likes of which has never been seen before, and these are the signs to look for that tell us our Lord's return is upon us. A world driven þy fear—this is how the Bible says things will be when Jesus returns. So until He does return to fix the mess, times are going to be more challenging than ever before, in many ways on many fronts. You're going to *need* God's peace in the future, so make the decision now to cultivate and protect it!

> *Pursue peace with all people, and holiness, without which no one will see the Lord.*

—HEBREWS 12:14

To pursue peace means to follow after peace. To pursue someone means to follow them and go where they go. If they go straight, we go straight. If they turn left, we turn left. If they stop, we stop. We do that because we're following them.

If we're told to be led forth with peace, that means we're to let peace guide us. We're to let peace be the final say in deciding what to say or do. Why? Because if living peace has the inherent power to guard our hearts and minds, we ought to realize that it also has the inherent power to lead us according to God's perfect will for our lives. Praise God! Peace doesn't follow us—we follow it.

CHAPTER 6

Three Elements
of Peace

G od's living peace has three basic, fundamental elements. Each one is very important and all three are needed if we're to live a victorious life in Christ. First, God's living peace is a statement of faith. Second, that same living peace protects us from fear. Third, God's living peace is to be given away.

1. Peace Is a Statement of Faith

Hebrews 11:6 says that without faith, it's impossible to please God. Since we're made in His image and likeness, He expects us to live by faith like Jesus did. Many times in Scripture, we're told to walk by faith and not by sight. Throughout the Bible, God tells us to be people of strong faith. To show us how it's to be done, He gives us the four Gospels. He lets us see how His Son, Jesus, lived and ministered in faith. In other words, He gives us the perfect standard by which to measure our growth.

When we study the life and ministry of Jesus, we not only see a Man of great faith, but we see a Man of tremendous peace. Nothing phased the Lord! His peace was in control of every situation—no exceptions. He was a Man of great faith and great peace because one can't exist without the other. God designed them to function together. It's impossible to walk in faith and not be in peace, and equally impossible to be at peace without walking in faith.

Many fail to realize that when they lose their peace, they've lost their faith. Peace is there when a person is truly living by faith. If our peace is gone, it's because our faith has departed as well. When our faith departs, fear comes in to replace it and Satan gains the upper hand against us.

Dr. Doyle (Buddy) Harrison was my father in the faith before his homegoing in 1998. Once, when discussing this issue of divine peace with him, he made a great statement which has helped me to maintain peace in times of intense satanic attack. *He said there is always peace in knowing!* That is, if we know the Word, and know that God knows our heart, peace rules and reigns because faith comes by hearing, and hearing by the Word of God. (Romans 10:17)

As we take time to meditate in the promises which cover our situation, our faith is energized and God's living peace gains control. It's when we allow the unknown to dominate our thoughts that fear comes in like a flood against us. *Stay with what we know!* We know God and we know His Word. Praise God! We know He loves us more than we can imagine and that He watches over His Word to perform it. (See Jeremiah 1:12.) That brings peace! If we stay with those truths, fear won't be able to create havoc in our hearts and minds.

We confess the Word because it brings faith to our hearts, which brings the manifested peace of God, but confessing the Word isn't magical. We've got to believe what we're confessing. There's the confession *unto* faith, and then there's the confession *of* faith. Although we might need to confess to get faith, we must have faith to confess what we truly believe in our hearts. How do we know when we've made the transition? When peace rules and reigns in our hearts! *When peace comes, it means we've gone from confession to get faith, to confession of what we truly believe.* It becomes a confession of faith.

A person's decision to believe God will lead them to a place of peace. Look to Jesus to see how it's done, because His faith was the most developed of anybody who has ever lived on earth. We never see Jesus anxious or out of control. He was never in distress or pressured about anything, nor anxious over any situation He faced, no matter how unraveled the people around Him were.

Because Jesus really understood the truth we read in Philippians 4:19, He knew that God would always be there for Him to provide whatever was needed for the moment. It didn't matter what was needed, Jesus knew His Father would be there on time. Whether it was feeding thousands of hungry people in the desert with only a few fish and pieces of bread, the power needed to heal the multitudes of sick, or the wisdom to give an answer to save a prostitute from being stoned to death in John 8:7, Jesus was at peace. He had the knowledge of who God was in His life and ministry.

Do we ever see Jesus nervously pacing the floor, confessing Philippians 4:19 because He's not convinced God is going to come through? Do we ever see Jesus trying to work up His faith, confessing the promises of God to convince Himself that God is really going to come through in a clutch? Never! Jesus said that the works He did, we can do also. (John 14:12-14) That doesn't just mean miracles.

That runs the gamut and deals with every aspect of His earthly ministry.

Did Jesus ever get upset or angry? Sure! He got upset with His staff over their spiritual thickness and lack of faith on more than one occasion (see Mark 8:14-21; 9:19). He also got angry with the hypocrisies coming forth from the Pharisees and Sadducees (see Matthew 21:12; Mark 11:15; John 2:15). There's no doubt our Lord was furious when He took time to fashion a whip from cords, and then used that whip to drive out hundreds of people and animals from the temple—overturning tables, chairs, and birdcages in the process. But even in those moments of anger, exasperation, and frustration, Jesus maintained a level of inner peace that enabled Him to keep these outbursts measured, in check, and in perspective to the bigger picture of Who He was, and Who He was serving. We must learn how to do the same!

God's Peace Will Silence Any Storm

In Jesus' ministry, we see that several notable miracles took place when He was crossing the sea of Galilee.

On the same day, when evening had come, He said to them, "Let us cross over to the other side."

Now when they had left the multitude, they took Him along in the boat as He was. And other little boats were also with Him.

And a great windstorm arose, and the waves beat into the boat, so that it was already filling.

But He was in the stern, asleep on a pillow. And they awoke Him and said to Him, "Teacher, do You not care that we are perishing?"

Then He arose and rebuked the wind, and said to the sea, "Peace, be still!" And the wind ceased and there was a great calm.

But He said to them, "Why are you so fearful? How is it that you have no faith?"

And they feared exceedingly, and said to one another, "Who can this be, that even the wind and the sea obey Him!"

—MARK 4:35-41

The main issue in this story is faith. Jesus had it and the disciples didn't. We know this because when Jesus finished rebuking the elements, He turned to His men and scolded them for having no faith. The reason they had no faith was because their hearts and minds were unprotected. They had lost their faith because they had lost their peace. They followed what they saw with their eyes and felt with their feelings. They saw the waves. They felt the wind and rain. They saw the boat filling up with water. What they saw caused them to lose their peace, and thus lose their faith. The peace of God, designed to guard their hearts and minds, was overcome by the fear that gripped them.

On the other hand, we see Jesus at total peace with Himself and with the situation. Remember, He was in the same boat as the disciples. He saw the same waves, felt the same wind and rain, and saw the water filling the boat just like His disciples did. What was the difference? He was operating in faith, and thus in peace, while the disciples were in fear for their lives.

The first thing to notice is that Jesus was so at peace in His relationship with God, He was sound asleep at the back of the boat. His disciples were in the front of the boat screaming in terror, overcome with fear for their lives, while at the same time, Jesus was sleeping like a baby! In fact, He was sleeping so soundly, they had to shake Him to wake Him! What an illustration of the power of peace in an individual's life! Here is their boat, being tossed all over the sea, filling up with water, and the disciples in utter fear and panic for their lives. At the same time in the same boat, we see another Man. This Man is different than the rest. This Man knows God and the power of His own words.

Jesus didn't tell His disciples to go halfway and drown! No, He told them to go to the other side. That was His Word, and that was the way it was going to be. Having said that, He went to sleep. He had faith in God and His Word; therefore, He went to sleep in peace.

However, while He was sleeping, a giant windstorm came across the lake and caught everybody by surprise. Now many in the boat that day were professional fishermen who had done their fishing on the same sea of Galilee. They had seen storms before, but this one was different. It was demonic. It was quick, sudden, and terrifying. Isn't that how the devil tries to come against us? He attacks with no warning and with an intensity that overwhelms us if we're not prepared for it.

The Power of Spoken Peace

When the disciples finally awakened Jesus, He went to the front of the boat and spoke three words. *Peace, be still!* Why? For two reasons. First, because He only spoke what God told Him to say. Psalm 85:8 says that God speaks peace to His people, so Jesus was following after the example of His Father God. Second, Matthew 12:34 says that out of the abundance of the heart, the mouth will speak. Jesus was filled with God's living peace, so that is what came rolling out of His mouth in this time of crisis.

How many times did Jesus say He only spoke what God told Him to say? If we look at John 5:19, John 12:49-50, and John 14:24, we see that Jesus trained Himself to say only what He heard His Father say, or what His Father told Him to say. If He spoke peace to the problem, He did so because God told Him to. And why did God tell Him to?

I will hear what God the Lord will speak, for He will speak peace to His people and to His saints.

—PSALM 85:8

God told us in the Old Testament that He spoke peace when necessary. Jesus studied the Old Testament scriptures and knew them better than anyone ever has or ever will. He knew that God spoke peace to His people and, therefore, He had a scriptural foundation for what He did in the boat as they faced the raging storm. In addition, He only said what God told Him to say, so we know it was God who told Him to speak peace to the problem.

In the Greek, the word translated "peace" in Mark 4:39 means silence; to be calm. (See *Strong's Exhaustive Concordance of the Bible*, #4623.) In other words, Jesus was using His faith in such a way so as to bring quiet and calm to this wild and unruly sea. How did He do that? By speaking peace to the problem. Oh, praise God! Can you begin to see the power in speaking peace to your problems?

Jesus spoke peace to the storm because He knew the power generated in speaking peace to the attacks against Him and His disciples. Many teachers have studied this story and looked only at the power of spoken faith, but we can see it today in a new light. Understand the power of spoken peace! *Learn to speak peace to your problem, because it's a statement of faith.* Follow the example given by our Lord Jesus. Of all the things He could have said in that situation, He chose to speak peace to the storm. There is power in spoken peace! The power of God's peace has the inherent power to calm any storm Satan brings against us. If we're really walking in faith, we'll be speaking peace to our problems. We'll learn to speak peace to the raging wind and sea, and see that peace calm the elements in Jesus' name.

When Jesus stood in the bow of the boat, He did not say, "Be quiet! Stop blowing! Quit raining! Do you know who I am? I'm the Son of Almighty God!" He didn't say, "Waves, stop crashing against our ship!" He didn't say, "Wind, stop blowing!" He didn't say, "Father God, please get us out of this mess before we all sink and drown!" No, He chose to speak three simple words. "Peace, be still!" Words full of faith and peace! The storm He saw with His eyes and felt with His senses was no problem for Him. He had the peace of God guarding His heart and mind. Therefore, He could use it to speak forth God's power and calm the storm in a moment of time.

Can we do that today? In John 14:12, Jesus said we could. "Most assuredly, I say to you, he who believes in Me, the works that I do he will do also; and greater works than these he will do, because I go to My Father." How can Jesus make this amazing statement about us? Because that same peace that was evident in Him that day on the lake is the same peace available to us today through the indwelling presence of the Holy Spirit. We just have to decide to let it rule and dominate, like Jesus did.

I've been in situations like Jesus and His disciples. Since 1980, I've been doing missions work in the Philippines. For the first seven or eight years, I operated in the offices of evangelist and teacher. After proving myself faithful to God in those offices for that season of time, He moved me into the apostolic office I have operated in ever since. These are not stationery ministry gifts that primarily operate in one set location, like that of a pastor. They are mobile in nature and function. Therefore, to do what I'm called to do in the five-fold ministry offices I've stood in (see Ephesians 4:12) or stand in today, I must travel extensively. And when you travel extensively in the Philippines, many times you'll be traveling by boat.

The Philippines is an island nation comprised of more than 7,100 islands. Most of the islands are uninhabited. The majority of the population lives on only five or six major islands. Over the years, I've traveled by boat from island to island thousands of times to minister. And when I say travel by boat, I'm talking about boats of all different shapes and sizes.

In most cases, the boats leave port at 7:00 p.m. and arrive in port at 7:00 a.m. the next morning. That's at least a 12-hour boat ride in the night across the high seas. Many times we've been out there getting buffeted by high winds, driving rain, and giant waves. I know what it's like to be out in the open sea in a small boat with big waves hitting the ship.

If you let it, the experience can be terrifying. I've been on boats when the sea was so rough, the bow of the boat would almost disappear underneath the waves. The boat would go over to the left and almost capsize, then go over to the right and almost capsize again. It's easy for us to sit in the comfort of our living room and read about this incident in Mark 4:35-41. But I've been out there like they were, and I can tell you that when a boat full of people is getting tossed around on the open sea, fear is so tangible you can cut it with a knife.

To heighten the element of fear, notice that when Jesus and His disciples left the shore to go to the other side, it was evening. That means that by the time they got out into the middle of the lake, it was nighttime. That means it was dark!

Like Jesus and His disciples that night on the sea of Galilee, most of my voyages in the Philippines have been at night. It's bad enough when the ocean is rough and the boat is getting tossed around like a cork, but it's even more tempting to fear when it's happening in the dark of night.

I can appreciate their situation that night. I can understand how tempted they were to yield to their fears. I've been out there with hundreds of people screaming, praying the rosary, crying, clutching their children or belongings, and fighting over the life preservers. They're afraid for their lives—just like the disciples were that night in the boat with Jesus.

How strong would our faith be in a situation like that? "Well, Apostle Mike, I believe I would have done it right. I believe the Word, and I'd be confessing the scriptures." Are you sure? It's really frightening when you're in the midst of it and people are panicking all around you. People throwing up all over themselves for the roughness of the sea, or clinging to their bunks for dear life—fearful they're going to get swept overboard by some giant wave.

Let me tell you, in times like that, all kinds of thoughts are running through your mind, and none of them glorify God! Who knows? Had it been you and I out there that night with Jesus, maybe we would have caved in to fear sooner than His disciples did.

Two Groups in One Boat

To look at this story in terms of faith, understand that there were two groups in that boat at the same time. In the front of the boat we have the disciples of the Lord. They're terrified and gripped with fear for their lives. In the back of the boat we have Jesus. He's so at peace that He's sound asleep.

The waves are hitting the back of the boat just as much as they're hitting the front of the boat. The wind is blowing at the back of the boat just as much as it is blowing at the front of the boat. It's not like we have a raging storm at the front half of the boat and calm, balmy conditions at the back half of the boat.

The storm was coming against Jesus the same as it was coming against His men. But look at and appreciate the difference in how the front half and the back half of the boat responded to the same set of circumstances. Those at the front of the boat were full of fear; the One at the back of the boat was full of faith!

When Jesus went to the front of the boat, His faith drove out the fear—not the other way around. How could that happen? Because Jesus was in peace and that peace was guarding His heart and mind, just like it will do for us if we will let it.

When the disciples went to the back of the boat, they took their fear with them, but it didn't have any affect on Jesus. God's peace was guarding His heart and mind to such an extent, Satan had no way in to put his fears upon Jesus. Instead, Jesus took His faith and used it to drive out the fear.

First, He drove it out of the back of the boat, where the disciples had brought it. Second, He drove it out of the front of the boat, where it had camped since the storm had come. Third, He drove it off the lake with a faith command using three words of spoken peace. *I want to be like Jesus.* How about you?

In the Philippines, thousands of lives are lost each year to ship sinkings. So, when you're out there at night and the storms are raging all around you in your little boat, the devil bombards your mind with thoughts of disaster and death. How can we cast down such thoughts while our five senses tell us there is no hope? By letting the peace of God rule and reign, just like Jesus did.

Jesus was so close to God and so full of His Word, His mouth spoke out what was in His heart in abundance. He heard God tell Him what to say, and He said it with faith, confidence, and authority. We need to develop an understanding about peace to such a degree that we can do the same things Jesus did in the boat that night. I don't want to be like those disciples anymore, holding on for dear life while pleading in fear for God to come and do something—anything—to deliver them from their situation. We can do it! It is possible! It can be done!

Peace Causes Us to Walk on Water

Three separate accounts in Matthew 14:22-33, Mark 6:45-51, and John 6:15-21, show another tremendous example of the power of God's living peace in the ministry of Jesus. In this story, we're once again out on the sea of Galilee, but this time Jesus is not in the boat with His men. He's walking on the water, coming towards His disciples who have been told to row to the other side of the lake. The contrast between Jesus and His men is once again very stark.

We see the disciples rowing for all they're worth, going nowhere, because it says they were rowing against the wind. Then we see Jesus effortlessly walking on the water, coming towards them in the boat.

At this point, many believers look for excuses to justify failure. They say that only Jesus could do these things because He was the Son of God. But remember that we're sons and daughters of God too, and God loves us just as much as He loves Jesus. (See John 17:23.) If we're born again, we have the same Holy Spirit in us as Jesus did. Furthermore, when Jesus gave the command for Peter to step out of the boat and walk to Him, he did!

> *And Peter answered Him and said, "Lord if it is You, command me to come to You on the water." So He said, "Come." And when Peter had come down out of the boat, he walked on the water to go to Jesus.*

—MATTHEW 14:28-29

Peter wasn't even born again, but still he was able to step out and walk on the water. If Peter can do it, we can too. He was a servant of the Most High God, but at that point in his life, he wasn't saved. He didn't have the Holy Spirit living in his heart like we do now. So if he could do it in simple faith, how much more could we do it if we needed to?

Understand that when we talk about walking on the water, the "water" doesn't just refer to bodies of water like the Sea of Galilee. Spiritually, it represents the testings, temptations, and trials of the enemy. In our Lord's case here, the water itself was part of the problem, but for us today, our problems are financial, physical, mental, emotional, marital, spiritual, and so forth. To walk on the water means to rise above the problems and be victorious over them. If we allow God's living peace to dominate our lives like Jesus did, we'll have the faith to walk on the water. We'll have the faith to tackle any problem successfully.

In Matthew's account of this story, he says that when Peter saw the boisterous wind and the large waves, he got scared and began to sink. In other words, fear replaced faith and Peter lost his peace. But then Jesus reached out, caught Peter by the arm, and pulled him back up on top of the water.

It was here, while Jesus and Peter were standing on the water in the middle of the lake, that Jesus conducted a

Bible study on the subject of faith. The wind was still blowing. The waves were still high and dangerous. Yet Jesus was so at peace and in faith, He was totally oblivious to the conditions around Him. In the midst of all that, He took a few moments to teach Peter about faith and corrected him for allowing doubt to come in, causing him to sink. What an example to follow!

Think about it. Here we see Jesus and Peter, talking about faith while they're strolling along on top of the water. To Jesus, it was no different than taking a stroll through the neighborhood on a Sunday afternoon. Jesus was so consumed with living peace from God, He acted like the wind and waves weren't even there. His heart and mind were so guarded by God's peace, it was like the weather became a non-issue. We can let God's living peace take us to that level of faith. It's only a matter of commitment. *Our free will can take us there if we want it badly enough.*

Jesus was so detached from the wind and water, He fully intended to pass the boat and finish crossing the lake on foot! Mark 6:48 says that when Jesus came towards them as they were rowing in the boat, he would have passed them by. To Him, it was like they weren't even there! Our Lord was so focused in faith and peace, He didn't even intend to stop when he reached the boat in which His men were rowing.

Like Jesus, we can come to the place in this life where we're so at peace with God, we become oblivious to the circumstances around us that contradict the Word of God. Just like when Jesus walked on the water, we can walk above the pain, the physical symptoms, the negative medical reports, the financial obstacles, the lies and backbiting from others, and so forth. The peace of God, when in control of our lives, will lift us up and cause us to ride on the high places of the earth. That is why this subject is so important to understand.

When we allow God's peace to rule and dominate like it did for Jesus, we'll stand steadfast in the midst of the testings, temptations, and trials. We won't waiver, doubt, or yield to double-mindedness. The power of God will carry us through to victory—sometimes so suddenly that we have to pinch ourselves to see if we're not dreaming.

As an example, look once again at this story about Jesus crossing the lake on foot. We see from John 6:21 that when Jesus and Peter climbed back into the boat, the boat was immediately at the other side of the lake. Suddenly! Victory in the blink of an eye! *This was the Lord's doing; It is marvelous in our eyes* (Psalm 118:23).

Many times in the Bible, we see God moving suddenly to deliver His people. It may look like nothing is happening, but don't lose heart! It only takes God a split second of time to bring victory to us. The disciples were rowing with futility, going nowhere in their own strength against the wind. But in the time it took them to blink their eyes, they were out of that situation, across the lake, and at dry land!

That's what God's peace will do for us. It will put God in a position to do miraculous things on our behalf, because peace is a statement of faith, and faith is what allows God to do what needs to be done in our lives.

2. Peace Protects Us From Fear

To understand peace as a statement of faith, we must see how fear comes to rob us of our faith and peace. But now, let's look from a different perspective: How peace protects us from fear in a greater way.

Be anxious for nothing, but in everything by prayer and supplication, with thanksgiving, let your requests be made known to God; and the peace of God, which surpasses all understanding, will guard your hearts and minds through Christ Jesus.

—PHILIPPIANS 4:6-7

To be anxious for nothing means not to worry about anything. Some might say that it's impossible to live a worry-free life, but if that's true, God lied when He told us to be anxious about nothing. God would be unjust with us if He told us to do something He knew we couldn't do. We can live worry-free, but only if we follow the Word of God and utilize the weaponry made available to us by God.

Once we bring our situation to God in prayer, we're to believe He hears and answers us.

Now this is the confidence that we have in Him, that if we ask anything according to His will, He hears us. And if we know that He hears us, whatever we ask, we know that we have the petitions that we have asked of Him.

—1 JOHN 5:14-15

Releasing our faith at that point, we're to then let God's peace guard and protect our hearts and minds. It's our choice once again. Satan will come against us—we can be sure of that. He'll try to sow fear into our minds with rapid-fire thoughts that attempt to overwhelm and control us. Physical symptoms or negative external circumstances may be there as well.

The only way to effectively guard our hearts and minds is to let the living peace of God dominate. As we said before, it's the divine antidote to enable us to fight off the fear that comes against our hearts and minds.

When Jesus was in the boat with His disciples in Mark 4:35-41, His peace effectively dealt with the fear that collectively gripped the hearts and minds of the disciples. Even though many of the men in that boat with Him were professional fishermen, they were still overcome with fear by what their senses told them. Big storm. Little boat. No way out! But while they were coming apart at the seams, Jesus remained calm and in complete control of Himself and the situation. God's living peace protected Jesus from being influenced by the fear His men felt.

Jesus spoke peace to the wind and waves and did not allow the fear of His disciples to affect His faith. Jesus spoke peace to Peter as He pulled him up out of the water, and He didn't let Peter's cry of fear affect His faith.

> *Now may the God of peace Himself sanctify you completely; and may your whole spirit, soul, and body be preserved blameless at the coming of our Lord Jesus Christ.*

> —1 THESSALONIANS 5:23

God is called a God of peace because, as we see in this passage, He uses His peace to separate (sanctify) us from fear—spirit, soul, and body. God's peace separates us from fear. Legally, it separates us from the fear of going to hell for all eternity. In a living sense, it separates us from the attacks that come against us daily.

God's peace creates a gulf between us and the devil which his fear cannot penetrate. No matter what kind of fear we're talking about, God's peace has the power to neutralize it.

Peace Conquers the Fear of Death

Hebrews 2:14-15 says that Jesus came to destroy him who had the power of death, that is, the devil. In doing this,

Jesus released man from lifetime bondage to the fear of death. I believe these scriptures are telling us that the fear of death is the root of all fear. Therefore, when Jesus came to save us from death, it was the fear of death He sought to destroy. He knew He needed to go to the root of all fear and deal effectively with the problem at that point.

Stop and think about it. Examine every fear you have and see if it doesn't tie into the fear of death. Fear of death can be seen in a fear of losing something important to you, such as finances or a job, or in a fear of disease or physical harm from an accident or crime—in other words, the end or "death" of something in your life.

I have found that directly or indirectly, the fear of death is behind all the fears that grip us and hold us under the devil's dominion. When Jesus left us with His peace, He did so knowing that it had the ability to set us free from the fear of death.

Legal peace takes away our fear of impending eternal judgment, but if we're not careful, the fear of death can creep back into our lives and regain the upper hand. It's not that we've lost our salvation, but that we've allowed fear to once again have a place in our hearts and minds. The good news for us is that when God's peace is in control of our lives, we proportionately eliminate the fear of death and it has no place in us.

Death is something that terrifies man because it's an evil that we can't run from. In any form, death was never a part of God's plan for man. We instinctively recoil from death, because it is the result of sin, which we must now experience because of Adam's sin in the Garden of Eden. Although death is an enemy God never intended for us to face, it's the last enemy that will be put under the feet of our Lord Jesus. (1 Corinthians 15:26)

When Adam sinned, the first thing that left was the indwelling presence of the Holy Spirit. God's peace departed with Him. We know that, because when God went looking for Adam and Eve after they sinned, they were hiding because they were afraid. (Genesis 3:10) Sin gave the devil legal permission to come in, and when he did he brought fear with him. Satan's fear replaced the peace and tranquility of the Garden. Death had come, and the fear of death had come with it.

Thank God we can now enjoy a life free from the fear of death and any and all fears that spring from it. Death is no longer something to be feared. If we understand it in light of our legal peace with God, it's actually something to look forward to. Death is our homecoming—our passage into the spirit world to be with our heavenly Father forever. And even if we face death at some point before our appointed time, we can face it in peace. It's not something to fear anymore.

Not having a fear of death gives us the ability to enjoy life and to be utilized by God to the maximum extent. God's peace surrounds us and separates us from the fear which holds most of the human race in bondage. We become like those mentioned in Hebrews 11. No matter who they were, where they lived, or how they died, they died in faith. (Hebrews 11:13) That means they died in peace—even if they never received the full manifestation of the promises of God they stood for in faith!

Dr. Buddy Harrison made this observation, which opened my eyes and set me free in this area. People can die in faith without ever actually seeing God's promise to them fully come to pass. This may be a surprising statement to some believers, but look carefully at Hebrews 11 and see who's being talked about in that passage—people like Abraham, Enoch, Noah, Joseph, Jacob, Moses, Joshua, David, and others.

Are we going to say these guys had no faith? The Bible says in Hebrews 11:13, "these all died in faith, not having received the promises, but having seen them afar off were assured of them and embraced them. . . ." What does that mean? It means they understood the promise of God, believed it, and stood in faith for it—but didn't see it in their lifetime.

They lived in faith; therefore, they lived in peace. It also means they died in faith, therefore, they died in peace. The fear of death never got a hold of them. Even though they embraced a promise which did not come to pass fully at that time, they remained steadfast in faith and peace. Whether they died before their appointed time or not is not the issue. The important truth to see here is that they gave glory to God right up to the day they died—with their faith walking in the peace of God.

Can we do this? It's one thing to say we're not afraid to die when we're not facing death. But when death is knocking on the door, and by all indications it looks like we are going to die, can we still walk in faith and peace?

Consider Stephen, who died with the glory of God on his face. (Acts 7:54-60) According to 1 Corinthians 15:55-57, we know there is no more sting to death. Jesus removed it through His death and resurrection.

This is the kind of power the peace of God gives to us, and that's the kind of revelation that keeps us shouting the victory all the days of our lives.

3. Peace Is Given by God to Be Given Away

God expects us to share His living peace with others. With our words and our very presence, we're to speak and impart peace into the lives of those we deal with daily. That's why it's important to let God's peace separate us from the fear of death. We need to be free so God can use us to set others free. We have to be walking in the light of God's living peace before we can effectively offer it to others. But if we're bound up with fear in our lives, we can't very well speak peace into the lives of others, can we?

As we walk in the power of God's living peace to a greater degree, we're able to influence others more and more with that same peace. We become like Jesus, by having the peace which rules our lives take control of any situation in which we find ourselves. No matter what it was that Jesus walked into, God's peace flowing through Him exerted the power to change the situation for the glory of God. The good news is that we can do the same. The sobering news is that we're responsible to do it!

In the story where Jesus raises Jairus' daughter back to life, use your imagination to see how our Lord's peace gave comfort and strength to Jairus when he learned that his daughter had already died.

> And behold, one of the rulers of the synagogue came, Jairus by name. And when he saw Him, he fell at His feet and begged Him earnestly, saying, "My little daughter lies at the point of death. Come and lay Your hands on her, that she may be healed, and she will live."
>
> While He was still speaking, some came from the ruler of the synagogue's house who said, "Your daughter is dead. Why trouble the Teacher any further?"
>
> As soon as Jesus heard the word that was spoken, He said to the ruler of the synagogue, "Do not be afraid; only believe."

—MARK 5:22-23,35-36

Try to imagine the shock, grief, and remorse of Jairus as his servants greeted him with the news about the death of his precious daughter. Moments before, he was a man full of hope, heading back to his daughter with the Man who was both willing and able to heal her from this terminal illness. But it was too late! The news was given—don't bother Jesus anymore, your daughter has already died.

Put yourself in his position, especially if you have children. How would you feel if it were you instead of Jairus, and your son or daughter instead of his? No doubt we'd be torn to emotional pieces, just like Jairus was. Heading home with Jesus, so excited and filled with hope for the healing of his little girl—only to have those hopes dashed with the news of her death.

But listen to what Jesus said as He heard the report about Jairus' daughter. *Do not be afraid; only believe!* Looking straight into the eyes of Jairus, Jesus spoke with such a tone of confidence, surety, calmness, and authority. His words immediately replaced fear and sorrow with hope, excitement, and renewed anticipation. These few words spoken with faith and peace immediately reversed the anguish of the moment. Spoken peace has the power to do that, because God Himself is the force which backs the statements of faith we make.

There had to be a thousand thoughts running through the mind of Jairus. First he hears that his daughter has died. He starts to grieve, but in the next breath, he hears Jesus say not to be afraid, but to only believe. What should he say? How should he respond? His daughter is dead and he's trying to deal with that. But on the other hand, why does Jesus still want to come to his house to pray for her? Why would He do that?

Maybe Jesus knows something about God's power that Jairus doesn't know. Why would Jesus say not to be afraid?

And why does He sound so confident and so sure? If she's dead there is nothing more anyone can do, right? But then why is Jesus still going to pray for her? You can imagine that Jairus must have been an emotional basket case by the time they all got back to his house.

What was Jesus doing when he told Jairus not to be afraid, but to only believe? He was giving away the peace that rules and reigns in His life and ministry. He was doing what God wanted Him to do. He was imparting living peace that would help Jairus move from a place of fear to a place of faith. Jesus was using His peace to change the atmosphere. He was imparting peace to give hope to a man who had just had all his hopes taken away. Jesus was using the peace of God to usher everyone there into the presence of God. In sharing the living peace of God, Jesus was giving that peace a chance to replace Jairus' fear with faith and hope.

Give Your Peace Away

Remember John 14:12. The works Jesus did are to be our works also. That means we're to impart God's living peace like Jesus did. When we encounter people like Jairus— people who have lost all hope—we can change things for the glory of God. We can share the peace of God which we have, just like Jesus did. Jesus did it, He taught His disciples to do it, and we should be doing it too.

> *The things which you learned and received and heard and saw in me, these do, and the God of peace will be with you.*
>
> —PHILIPPIANS 4:9

Our God of peace will be with us when we impart to others the living peace we have from God. Paul says they learned, which means he taught them. He says they received, which means he imparted spiritual gifts to them. They heard of him, which means Paul's reputation preceded him. And they saw, which means they watched Paul live a life dominated by the peace of God. Paul encouraged the Philippians to let the God of peace do the same things for them as He had done for him. They could then go out and effectively share Jesus in a way which would accurately represent Him to the lost.

Everyone in the body of Christ is entitled to enjoy this living peace from God, for our own good and the good of others. God's nature is one of giving. Since we're made in His image and likeness, our nature is to be just like His. As He gives to us, He expects us to give to others. If we're the recipients of God's living peace, we're obligated by His Word to esteem others more important than ourselves, and to share our peace with them. (Philippians 2:3-5)

CHAPTER 7

Peace Is a Fruit of the Human Spirit

But the fruit of the Spirit is love, joy, peace, longsuffer-
ing, kindness, goodness, faithfulness, gentleness, self-
control. Against such there is no law. And those who are
Christ's have crucified the flesh with its passions and desires.

—GALATIANS 5:22-24

The first thing we need to see here is that the peace in this passage is living peace, not legal peace. We're talking to people who belong to Christ, which means they're already born again. They've already received legal peace by virtue of the new birth. In these verses, Paul is teaching that once saved, the sanctifying work of the Holy Spirit begins to replace the works of the flesh with the fruit of the recreated human spirit. How fast that happens depends upon each person's commitment to excellence in Christ. Whether or not this spiritual growth and develop-ment takes place quickly, this is one of the major works of the Holy Spirit in the believer's life. He lives in us to help us become more and more like Jesus every day.

In Galatians 5, two lists are given. The first is a list of the works of the flesh. From verses 19 to 21, a number of things are specifically mentioned—adultery, fornication, unclean-ness, lewdness, idolatry, sorcery, hatred, contentions, jeal-ousies, outbursts of wrath, selfish ambitions, dissensions, heresies, envy, murders, drunkenness, revelries, and the like. The phrase "and the like" means there are other works of the flesh not listed here. However, this is a pretty good start!

Paul is teaching that when believers fail to grow, develop, and mature spiritually, these works of the flesh will continue to dominate their lives. But if they allow the Holy Spirit to lead them, and if they start walking in the Spirit and no longer in the flesh, they'll see the manifesta-tion of the second list, which is the fruit of the recreated human spirit.

Some teach that these fruits are the fruits of the Holy Spirit, but that is not true. The Holy Spirit doesn't need to bear fruit—we need to bear the fruit. In John 15:1-6, Jesus taught that He was the vine, and we, the born-again believ-ers, are the branches. The fruit grows on the branches, not on the vine or tree trunk.

If we read these verses in context, we see that the battle is between the old man and the new man. We are to put off the old, dead-to-sin flesh, and put on the new by letting the life and nature of God dominate the way we think, talk, and act. It's a contrast between what the dead flesh wants to continue to do, versus what the born-again spirit wants to do for God.

So these fruits are the fruits of our spirit man once we've become born-again children of God. They're to be developed in our lives so we can overcome and subdue the tendencies of the dead flesh. Notice that one of the nine fruits listed is peace—not legal peace, but living peace.

The Body of Christ Is to Function As a Team

Many of the works of the flesh deal with issues of the heart. This includes things like pride, jealousy, envy, selfish ambition, and conceit. The peace of God gives us the ability to overcome these things. We can walk in the Spirit because we're living in the Holy Spirit according to Galatians 5:25. To walk in the Spirit is to let the Holy Spirit dominate every area of our life. It means to follow the desires of our born-again spirit and no longer the dead-to-sin flesh we still live in. Among other things, it means to let the peace of God rule in our hearts and minds.

That's very important, because the body of Christ is supposed to function as a team. All of the members of the body have a part to play, and everybody's part is important. If we forget that world evangelism is a team game, we'll get ourselves involved in the works of the flesh again. There will be what we see listed in Galatians 5:19-21, with more jealousy, envy, competition, backbiting, murmuring, spreading rumors, gossiping, and other such activities. We'll see what is described in 1 Corinthians 12:12-27. The eye saying to the hand, "I don't need you!" The ear saying to the foot, "I don't need you!" In other words, everyone trying to be the superstar, failing to work unselfishly as a team. Developing living peace in our lives is vital in maintaining a good working relationship in the body of Christ.

God designed the body of Christ to function together with every person contributing. You see this taught in Romans 12:3-6, Ephesians 4:11-16, and in other passages also. That's why the devil works so hard to create division and strife among us. He knows we'll never operate like God intended if we're always fighting with one another. Sad to say though, that's exactly where most of us end up—divided into groups, organizations, denominations, or movements; unwilling to walk in peace toward others in the body of Christ. We've become very good at erecting our traditional, charismatic, fundamental, or word-of-faith walls around us. We're even better at making sure they stay fortified and impregnable. In many cases, our attitude toward other believers is wrong and plays right into the hands of the enemy.

We all think that we're right and everyone else is wrong. If they don't agree with us and admit that we're right and they're wrong, we won't have anything to do with them. That kind of mindset has been firmly entrenched in the body of Christ since the days of the early church, and most of us have failed to see that the devil is the architect behind it.

Now of course, when we're dealing with major doctrinal heresies, or false doctrines and erroneous teachings that create confusion and draw people away from Christ and His standards of morality, excellence and integrity, we must separate. The Bible, in many places, tells us to do so. But when we're endeavoring to walk out God's peace on a day-to-day basis, we really need to learn to give people some space! The gospel of peace is not some personal witch hunt, where we should feel obligated to go around correcting the world with regards to all the nit-picky areas in their lives that we disagree with. In 1 Peter 3:11, we're told *to seek peace and pursue it.* And Romans 12:18 tells us that if at all possible, we're to live *peaceably* with all men! Let's be doers of these words as often as possible!

How should we overcome the carnal tendency to walk in strife towards others in the body of Christ? Whether it be an issue over minor points of doctrine or personal issues between brethren, how do we come to the place where we walk in the Spirit and not in the works of the flesh? We must allow God's living peace to dominate. If you look at the nine fruits of the recreated human spirit, you'll see that peace is number three. You'll also see that they all deal with how to treat others around us in this life. It doesn't matter whether we're with people who are saved or unsaved. These fruits are to be the dominant characteristics we manifest in the world daily.

If living peace from God dominates our hearts and minds, we'll be able to rise above our flesh and deal with the brethren in a spiritually mature way. When in control, the living peace of God enables us to subdue the carnal tendency towards strife and keeps the atmosphere ripe for the move of the Spirit of God.

Peace Is a Preservative

Salt is good, but if the salt loses its flavor, how will you season it? Have salt in yourselves, and have peace with one another.

—MARK 9:50

Jesus said that if salt loses its savor, how can it ever be useful again? We're the salt He's talking about. In Matthew 5:13-14, Jesus called believers the salt of the earth and the light of the world. If we read this passage in Mark carefully, we'll see that when we quit walking in peace towards each other in the body of Christ, we lose our ability to be a spiritual preservative within the body of Christ and outside to the lost world.

Satan knows that God does not work for us in an atmosphere of strife. God is love, and if we read about the characteristics of His kind of love in 1 Corinthians 13:4-8, we'll see there is no room for arguing, pride, backbiting, whispering, rumor spreading, slander, and other related activities.

Those things are listed in Galatians 5 as being some of the works of the flesh.

To preserve right relationship with one another in the body of Christ, we need to be at peace with God, with ourselves, then with each other. This is for our sakes, and for the sake of the rest of the world.

Learn to Peacefully Disagree

We're never going to find doctrinal unity in the body of Christ. There will be disagreements over Bible doctrine right up to the day Jesus returns and sets us all straight. Don't misunderstand me, I'm all for unity whenever we can make it happen. That's the atmosphere God wants and works the best. But when folks disagree over Bible interpretation, you've got to analyze the disagreement and decide whether it's important enough to warrant a cessation of fellowship.

As an example, doctrines which deny the basic tenets of faith for salvation are major issues of disagreement. If someone is teaching salvation by works and not by faith, that is a major area of disagreement, and it might not be possible for fellowship to continue. But in most cases, the areas of disagreement between brethren deal with issues that do not directly affect a person's salvation, but rather are personal issues dealing with the affairs of this life.

As far as I'm concerned, if an issue of disagreement is not an issue which would affect a person's salvation, or condone obviously sinful lifestyles disguised as Christianity, I'm not going to let that disagreement hinder me in establishing a meaningful relationship with that brother or sister. Of course, it's a two-way street. If they won't fellowship with me, then there's nothing I can do about that. But at least from my perspective, I've done all I can to preserve unity within the body of Christ, and my conscience is clear before God. In other words, I have peace about the situation, knowing I've done everything I could to maintain peace between myself and other brethren in the body.

There will always be disagreement over minor areas of Bible interpretation, or disagreement in other areas concerning the affairs of this life. But we can't let those differences isolate us from each other and cut us off from God's flow. We have to let the peace of God preserve! We have to learn to walk in the Spirit and let the peace of God protect us from the destructive power of strife.

We're dreaming if we think we're all going to suddenly see our doctrinal errors, make the necessary adjustments, and write letters of apology to all the other groups, organizations, and denominations. In the same way, we're dreaming if we think everyone is suddenly going to wake up tomorrow, mature in their spirit, and follow the teachings of 1 Corinthians 13:4-8 to the letter in all cases with all people. That's never going to happen! But we're not responsible for everyone else—we're only responsible for our own personal lives. We need to walk in peace, be a preservative to the best of our ability, and give God the opportunity to use us the way He wants to. In my life and ministry for Jesus, I've always endeavored to give people the benefit of the doubt, and believe the best of people until proven otherwise. We've been taken advantage of because of that on more than one occasion, but because our hearts are right and we're seeking and pursuing God's peace, the Lord has always protected us and kept the enemy from using people to damage or destroy our work in the Lord.

For God is not the author of confusion but of peace, as in all the churches of the saints.

—1 CORINTHIANS 14:33

With all lowliness and gentleness, with longsuffering, bearing with one another in love, endeavoring to keep the unity of the Spirit in the bond of peace.

—EPHESIANS 4:2-3

And we urge you, brethren, to recognize those who labor among you, and are over you in the Lord and admonish you, and to esteem them very highly in love for their work's sake. Be at peace among yourselves.

—1 THESSALONIANS 5:12-13

For where envy and self-seeking exist, confusion and every evil thing are there. But the wisdom that is from above is first pure, then peaceable, gentle, willing to yield, full of mercy and good fruits, without partiality and without hypocrisy. Now the fruit of righteousness is sown in peace by those who make peace.

—JAMES 3:16-18

As a preservative, living peace from God protects our relationship with God and protects our ability to stay in faith and love with all the other brethren in the body of Christ. It puts us in a place where we can stay focused with others and concentrate only on the issues that really matter, which would be those that directly relate to soul-winning around the world. With peace in control, we can love others and work with them—no matter what group, organization, or denomination they may belong to.

CHAPTER 8

Let God's Peace
Introduce You

In the front of most Bibles, we'll find a listing of all the Old and New Testament books. Including the four Gospels, there are 27 New Testament books. Bear in mind that even though the four Gospels are included in the listing of New Testament books, most of those four books are not New Testament. The New Testament did not become a legal reality in heaven with God until Jesus rose from dead, ascended into heaven, and put His shed blood on the mercy seat. When He did that, the New Testament legally replaced the Old Testament. So everything in the four Gospels that is before our Lord's resurrection is Old Testament, and everything after His resurrection is New Testament. For the sake of what we're talking about here, let's not include the four Gospels when talking about the New Testament books.

If we then subtract those four books from the total of all the books listed as being New Testament, we have 23 books. This begins with the book of Acts and goes all the way through the book of Revelation.

If we study each of these books carefully, we'll discover that in 19 out of 23 books, the Holy Spirit inspired the writer to greet the brethren with a salutation of peace! If it's the Holy Spirit telling these men what to write, we begin to understand how important this is to God. Once again, notice it's right at the beginning of the letter which, according to the law of first mention, indicates the importance of peace in our lives and ministries. Let's look at the first of these, found in the book of Romans.

To all who are in Rome, beloved of God, called to be saints: Grace to you and peace from God our Father and the Lord Jesus Christ.

—ROMANS 1:7

Grace and peace be unto all of you! Twenty-three letters were written, and in 19 of them, we start out with a salutation like this. It would seem the Holy Spirit feels that it is important to greet the saints with peace. If He thinks it's important, it is! He thinks it's so important, He inspires these men to put this salutation right up front, right at the beginning of these 19 letters. We are to start with God's peace and move on from there. Peace is the foundation we build upon.

Like the greeting found in Romans 1:7, look and see similar greetings in the following places: 1 Corinthians 1:3, 2 Corinthians 1:2, Galatians 1:3, Ephesians 1:2, Philippians 1:2, Colossians 1:2, 1 Thessalonians 1:1, 2 Thessalonians 1:2, 1 Timothy 1:2, 2 Timothy 1:2, Titus 1:4, Philemon 3, 1 Peter 1:2, 2 Peter 1:2, 2 John 3, Jude 2, and Revelation 1:4.

When we see God's peace being mentioned at the beginning of all these New Testament books, we know God wants us to understand the importance of peace! Because we have legal and living peace, we're to greet each other in peace—walking in faith, not in fear. We're to be at peace with God and with ourselves so we can be blessed as peace-makers and as peace-proclaimers to the world. (See Matthew 5:9 and Romans 10:15.)

Greetings of Peace Started in the Old Testament

The practice of greeting people with peace is not new. It was done in the Old Testament long before and during our Lord's earthly ministry. Even though we have a better covenant, which is based upon better promises, those people understood peace much more than most of us do today. That's tragic, because if any generation needs to know about the power of God's peace, it would be ours.

No other generation has faced the social pressure and stress that we face in this day and age, simply because I believe our generation will be the one to welcome back the Lord Jesus Christ. (Matthew 24:3-14) We're coming to the close of this age of grace. If the people back then needed to understand the power of God's living peace, how much more for us now?

> *David sent ten young men; and David said to the young men, "Go up to Carmel, go to Nabal, and greet him in my name.*
>
> *"And thus you shall say to him who lives in prosperity: 'Peace be to you, peace to your house, and peace to all that you have!'"*
>
> —1 SAMUEL 25:5-6

David was doing business with this man Nabal. Even though Nabal is described in this passage as an unscrupulous man, David instructed his workers to greet him with peace. As David's official representatives, they were told to bless Nabal with a greeting of peace. Peace to Nabal, his house (family), and all that he had.

David did this because he understood the importance of sharing his peace with others. In dealing with the knowledge of God's nature and plan for mankind, it has been said that David was generations ahead of his time. I agree with that, and here's just one example to support that belief. As an Old Testament man, David had more revelation on the power of spoken peace than many of us do today in the New Testament. Read through the Psalms and see how the peace of God is the underlying theme in so many of them—most of which David wrote himself.

Jesus Taught These Things to His Disciples

Remember that Jesus was the last Old Testament prophet. His ministry was to fulfill the Mosaic Law, pay the price for our sins, rise from the dead, and get the New Testament ratified and put into force. As an Old Testament prophet, Jesus studied the Old Testament scriptures and knew them better than anyone has ever known them. At the tender age of twelve, he was in the temple, astounding the religious leaders with His questions and insight concerning the Word of God. (Luke 2:46-47) With all the insight and knowledge Jesus had, I find it significant that He specifically taught His disciples to represent Him in ministry with salutations of peace.

> *But whatever house you enter, first say, 'Peace to this house.' And if a son of peace is there, your peace will rest on it; if not, it will return to you.*

> —LUKE 10:5-6

And when you go into a household, greet it. If the household is worthy, let your peace come upon it. But if it is not worthy, let your peace return to you.

—MATTHEW 10:12-13

In these two passages, we see Luke and Matthew talking about the same set of instructions Jesus gave His disciples when they were sent out for ministry. Jesus taught His followers to impart their peace whenever they entered someone's house for ministry.

Also, notice that Jesus instructed them to do this first. The first thing they were told to do when entering the house was to greet it with peace. Not the last thing when walking out the door or at some point during their visit, but first, right at the beginning. We've already pointed out the significance of that. You've heard the old saying: First things first! In this case, that old saying agrees with scriptural truth.

They were taught to give away what Jesus had given to them and to do it first. Their peace had come from God, and they had the responsibility to share it wherever they went in the name of Jesus. They were told to be a blessing by bringing God's peace to whatever condition the family or household may have been in when they arrived. That's our responsibility today as well.

But do we carry out our responsibilities? Jesus said our peace is supposed to come upon the house when we greet people at the door. The trouble is most of us don't have any peace to offer! How can we give what we're not walking in the light of ourselves? If we're not enjoying the fullness of God's living peace, we're not going to think of saying "Peace to this house," when we first enter someone's home, are we? Why? Because it hasn't been that important to us before. If it's important to us and we're walking in the light of it, we'll be thinking along those lines when we walk into someone's house. Out of the abundance of the heart our mouth will speak, so if we're full of God's peace, speaking it forth when we first enter someone's house will become automatic.

When was the last time someone came to your house and greeted you the way David's servants greeted Nabal? I've been saved since September 21, 1978, and it's never happened to me that I can remember. No one has ever come to my house and as they walked in said, "Peace be to you, Apostle Mike. Peace be to your family, and to all that you have." On the other hand, I've rarely done it myself when I've gone to visit others in their homes. Why is that? Simply because we're not being taught to do it by our leaders. They're not teaching it because they don't understand the importance of doing it themselves. I'm guilty on both counts. I've not walked with understanding on this subject, and I've not taught it to others. But by God's grace, things are changing!

It is important! I need to speak a greeting of peace the way Jesus taught His disciples to. I need to teach it to others as a minister of the Gospel. Although we're not accustomed to doing it, we need to cultivate the habit of greeting people with the peace of God.

Will it sound funny or awkward when we first start greeting people with salutations of peace? Of course it will! None of us are used to doing it or hearing it. But the more we speak peace to others, the more peace will come back upon us. It's like anything else we give to God—we always get back much more than what we give. If we give peace when we visit or meet people through the course of the day, we'll get back peace in a much greater abundance.

Of course, people will look at us funny when we begin greeting them with God's peace. But after the initial shock wears off, many will really appreciate what you're attempting to impart to them and their household. And isn't that what we're supposed to be doing anyway? Everyone, including me, could stand more of God's peace around the house these days, and who better to impart it than you and I?

Greet the brethren first with God's peace. Let's give away what God has given to us. This is God's way of giving back to us even more of what we are already giving out in His name.

The Last Thing Jesus Did on Earth

And He led them out as far as Bethany, and He lifted up His hands and blessed them. Now it came to pass, while He blessed them, that He was parted from them and carried up into heaven.

—LUKE 24:50-51

The last thing Jesus did before ascending into heaven was to lift up His hands and bless His disciples. The Word says that He was parted from them as He blessed them, and was carried up into heaven. Therefore, this was His very last act before sitting down at the right hand of God.

Jesus knew that He was leaving for a long time (so far, about 2,000 years) and that He was turning the task of world evangelism over to us. He knew that He would not be back in person until He came to take His church home at the close of this dispensation. The Lord also knew the early church would experience intense persecution, and many of them would be murdered for their faith. He knew the devil would stop at nothing to stop this thing before it really got going. Knowing all of this as He did, we can be sure His last parting act was one of great significance.

What did He do? He blessed His disciples. But what does that mean? What does it mean to be blessed? What would that blessing include? The disciples might have walked away from the ascension site saying, "Praise God, we were blessed by Jesus!" But so what? What was the significance in Jesus choosing to bless them as His last parting act before ascending to sit at God's right hand in heaven? I wanted to know what Jesus gave them when He blessed them. When I went to the Lord for an answer, He took me to the book of Psalms.

> *The Lord will give strength to His people; the Lord will bless His people with peace.*

> —PSALM 29:11

What will the Lord bless His people with? Peace! If we're born again, we're His people. He said that when He blesses us, He'll do so by imparting more of His peace to us. Praise God! *According to this passage, when God gives us His strength, He does so by blessing us with His peace.*

The members of the early church needed God's strength to go through the persecution they'd be facing, including imprisonments, beatings, murders, intimidation, torture, and anything else the devil could attack them with. Read through the book of Acts and portions of the epistles to see how the early church suffered when they took the Gospel to the uttermost parts of the earth. Even today in many parts of the world, people are dying for their faith. They're being tortured, imprisoned, beaten, and murdered—just like those in the early church.

Jesus knew then, and knows now, how much of God's strength believers need when facing this kind of persecution, or any kind of persecution. That's why He chose to bless them with His peace. When He was with them, He kept them from Satan because He was their strength. (John

17:12) But because He knew He was going away, they would need to find God's strength in another way. They would need to be blessed with His peace.

Stop and think about it. If we let the peace of God rule in our lives daily, what can the devil do against us? Nothing! If God's living peace guards our hearts and minds, especially during times of persecution or turmoil, how can the devil have any place in our lives? He can't! Blessed with God's strength, we become strong in the Lord and in the power of His might. (Ephesians 6:10)

Manifested peace produces inner, spiritual joy, and the joy of the Lord is our strength. (Nehemiah 8:10) When we allow the living peace of God to come over us, joy will well up from deep within our spirit man. We'll be smiling, laughing, and in general feeling good about ourselves. I don't know about you, but in times of intense demonic attack, that's important to me!

The living peace of God gives us the ability to feel good about ourselves, feel good about the situation we're in, and feel good about God's power to deliver us and set us free. Joy comes forth as the peace of God surrounds us like a shield, producing the strength that Satan has no answer for.

Jesus knew the power in blessing His disciples with peace. That's why, of all the things He could have done as He was being parted from them, He chose to bless them with peace. Peace is a blessing from God! In this day and age, we need as much peace as possible.

Peace: The First and The Last

Peace is mentioned throughout the New Testament many times. Because it's the first thing we're taught to say when meeting people, and one of the first things mentioned in so many of the New Testament books, we need to understand the emphasis on peace being first; that is, peace being the foundation the whole Gospel is built upon.

Let's take another look at the ministry of Jesus after He rose from the dead, but before He went back to heaven. The first thing Jesus said to His disciples after being raised from the dead was, *Peace be with you!* When He came to them for the first time, He made that statement twice. When He returned eight days later, Thomas being with the others this time, He again greeted His disciples by saying, *Peace be with you!* Of all the things Jesus could have said to begin His conversation with them, He chose to talk about God's peace. As I've already pointed out earlier when we looked at this exchange between the Lord and His disciples, we need to understand the importance of doing this today.

In John 20:21 NASB, Jesus says, *"Peace be with you; as the Father has sent Me, so I also send you."* Notice how the Lord combines the impartation of God's peace with the business of being sent evangelistically into the world. Why does Jesus talk about peace and evangelism in the same statement to His disciples? Because we've got to be strong in the Lord if we're to effectively represent Jesus to a lost and dying world.

To be spiritually strong we need to be blessed of God. An impartation of God's living peace is the blessing we need! That's why the need for peace is mentioned before we're told to go out into all the world. Peace is the foundation our evangelistic efforts are built upon. In short, we can't go out and make a difference for God without allowing His peace to dominate every area of our lives. We can't help Jesus set others free if we are still in bondage to fear and worry.

In this very limited time frame—between His resurrection and ascension—see the emphasis our Lord puts upon the peace of God. Of the many things He could have chosen to highlight, He chose to highlight peace. The peace of God literally became bookends for our Lord's forty days on earth after His resurrection—at the beginning and right at the end.

Go back before the crucifixion and see Jesus teaching His disciples about proper greetings when out ministering. In Luke 10:5, Jesus teaches them and says, "But whatever house you enter, first say, 'Peace to this house.'" Notice again that they were taught to speak a greeting of peace first—not at some point during the fellowship or at the end when they're walking out the door. First! Remember the old saying, "First things first"?

That's why 19 out of 23 New Testament books begin with a greeting of peace in the first few verses. The truth is very clear when we take time to let the Holy Spirit show it to us. Peace is foundational! Over and over again peace is mentioned first or written about first. It's what we build upon because it's what God builds upon in our lives. Without it consistently operating in our lives, we become vulnerable to Satan's attacks and are unable to accurately represent Jesus in strength to the world.

Jesus Is Made unto Us Wisdom

In 1 Corinthians 1:30, the Bible tells us that Jesus is made unto us wisdom from God. From the book of Proverbs, we can begin to understand what that truth means to us.

Happy is the man who finds wisdom, and the man who gains understanding.

Her ways are ways of pleasantness, and all her paths are peace.

—PROVERBS 3:13,17

Why is the man happy when he finds wisdom? Because all of his paths are peace. When Jesus is Lord of our lives and Lord over our daily routine, He becomes our peace—not just in a legal sense, but in a vital, living sense as well. Jesus is peace, so to follow after Him is to follow after peace. It's wise to stay in God's peace by letting Jesus be Lord in every area of our lives—every day. That's walking in true biblical wisdom.

To walk in an unwise way is to walk out from under the protection of God's living peace. As a result, we lose our faith and go back to tackling our problems with natural, human strength. That only guarantees defeat! Only in the strength of God can we successfully repel the attacks of the enemy. The wise man not only recognizes that truth, but also understands that God's strength has His peace as its foundation.

The more we commune with Jesus, the wiser we are, and more of His peace is manifested in our daily lives. We're walking along on His pathway, not our own. Our pathway could be compared to some old, backwoods country road, while God's pathway could be compared to a brand new no-speed-limit superhighway. The old country road was built primarily for slow-moving cars or farm vehicles, while the superhighway is designed for fast cars cruising at high speeds. Why should we sit on some old tractor, barely topping 20 miles per hour and creating a cloud of dust, when we could be sailing along on God's superhighway, traveling just as fast as we can go? Praise God! His pathway is a pathway of peace.

Say Hello with Peace, Say Good-Bye with Peace

Earlier, we learned that in most of the New Testament books, the writers were inspired by God to greet those they wrote to with a salutation of peace. But in many of those same books, the Holy Spirit also inspired the writers to conclude their letter with encouraging words about the power of peace.

> *Finally, brethren, farewell. Become complete. Be of good comfort, be of one mind, live in peace, and the God of love and peace will be with you.*

> —2 CORINTHIANS 13:11

Live in peace, and the God of peace will be with you! What a simple yet profound truth! It's so simple and so basic that we've missed enjoying it in our lives. Similar statements are made at the close of these other New Testament letters: Romans 15:33, Romans 16:20, Galatians 6:16, Ephesians 6:23, 1 Thessalonians 5:23, 2 Thessalonians 3:16, Hebrews 13:20, 1 Peter 5:14, 2 Peter 3:14, and 3 John 14.

The subject of peace is found both at the beginning and at the end of these New Testament books. We are to say hello with peace and say good-bye with peace. We live in peace and the God of peace will be with us. I can just see God up in heaven, shaking His head in frustration at our inability to grasp the importance of this basic, fundamental truth. What more can He do in His Word to show us how important this is? How is it that we have failed to really understand the importance of peace in our daily affairs?

We have to make the decision to read the Word in a whole new light and let the Lord build His peace into our lives. It needs to be as important to us as it was when God inspired these men to write so much about it. Let's get into the Word of God and let the Holy Spirit open our hearts, minds, and eyes. We need to let Him teach us and guide us into all truth on the subject of peace. The choice is up to us. We can let our hearts be troubled or we can let the Lord's peace dominate our lives, which will spill over into the lives of those we meet every day. The Word of God holds the key, and we hold the Word of God. Let's do it!

.

CHAPTER 9

The Simplicity of Finding God's Peace through the Word

How do we go from understanding the importance of God's living, vital peace to making it a reality in our daily lives? The answer is simple. We spend time with God in praise, worship, and prayer, and in study and meditation of His Word. This was the secret to the power of the early church leaders despite intense attacks and persecution against them.

It was no accident that these men and women had the strength to stand strong in the midst of life-threatening persecution. They had learned how to tap into God's strength and peace.

> *But we will give ourselves continually to prayer and to the ministry of the word.*

> —Acts 6:4

The key word here is continually. They knew they needed to spend time in prayer and study of God's Word and be consistent with it. They followed the orders God gave Joshua thousands of years before.

> *This Book of the Law shall not depart from your mouth, but you shall meditate in it day and night, that you may observe to do according to all that is written in it. For then you will make your way prosperous, and then you will have good success.*

> —JOSHUA 1:8

"Day and night" means continually. For the leaders of the early Christian church, that meant spending time with God every day. They had to maintain their inner peace to overcome the temptation to renounce their faith to save their lives. Just because Jesus blessed them with peace when He ascended into heaven didn't mean they wouldn't have to take steps to stay strong in that peace daily. God's living peace is like anything else offered in His salvation package. It must be nourished, cultivated, and protected. It can grow, but it can also be lost if we don't make the effort to replenish it on a consistent basis.

When Paul told the Ephesian believers to be filled with the Spirit, he was writing to people who were not only saved, but filled with the Spirit as well. (Ephesians 5:18) When he wrote, he wrote in the continuous sense. In other words, he was telling them to be filled and continue to do what was necessary to stay filled. It's like refilling the gas tank in your car. Just because you bought your car with a full tank of gas in it doesn't mean you'll never have to fill it up again. In fact, the more you use your car, the more gas you'll have to put into the gas tank. So where do we go? Back to the gas station to fill up.

Spiritually speaking, we must do exactly the same thing with God's Word to keep ourselves built up and guarded with God's peace. (Author's note: for a more detailed teaching on this important subject, refer to my book *Be Strong! Stay Strong!*)

Consistent Time With God Is the Key

We must start with consistent time set aside for God and for study of His Word. Time with God must balance time spent in study of God's Word. If we fill our minds with knowledge about God through Bible study, but fail to spend significant time with Him personally, we'll lack the intimacy needed to put our knowledge of God to work effectively. In short, we are to spend time with God as much as we spend time in study about God in His Word.

With that in mind, understand that praise, worship, and prayer are the three most important things you can do each day. That's why Satan works so hard to influence our free will, to get us so busy or distracted that we don't have enough time to see to these three priorities each day. Everything in life takes time, because we live in a time-bound dimension.

We are told in 2 Timothy 2:4 not to be entangled with the affairs of this life. When we do, we leave ourselves with no time to spend with God or in His Word. The devil tries to manage our time by getting us to decide to become entangled with the affairs of this life. There's a big difference between taking care of the affairs of this life and becoming entangled in them. We must recognize our daily responsibilities, such as cooking, cleaning, shopping, going to work, going to school, and so forth. However, if we're not careful, these everyday responsibilities and routines can become entanglements to us. They'll rob us of the time we need each day to spend with God and in study of His Word.

> *No one engaged in warfare entangles himself with the*
> *affairs of this life, that he may please him who enlisted him*
> *as a soldier.*

—2 TIMOTHY 2:4

If we read this passage carefully, we'll see that it's not the devil who entangles us in the affairs of this life. We do it to ourselves. The devil can't make us spend our time unwisely. All he can do is try to influence us to make the wrong decisions ourselves. No one engaged in spiritual warfare entangles himself with the affairs of this life. We should take care of the affairs of this life, but never allow them to entangle us.

What is an entanglement? It is anything that prevents us from fulfilling our spiritual priorities on a daily basis. Praise, worship, and prayer are the top three spiritual priorities we have. They're most important because they establish our communion with God. We need to know God before knowledge about God becomes helpful in our lives. That's why Satan works so hard to get us to put the affairs of this life ahead of the time we need with God. He knows that he can't defeat us just because he wants to. He has to maneuver us into a position where we defeat ourselves! When we make the wrong decisions with our time, we become entangled in the affairs of this life. It steals our time away from God, leaving us weak and unable to successfully resist the attacks of the enemy.

Remember, entanglements don't have to be sinful. They can be, but they don't have to be. There are many things we can choose to do with our time each day that are not sinful, but still take us away from God and His Word. According to Hebrews 12:1, entanglements are in two basic categories—weights and sins. Weights are things that are not sinful in and of themselves, but things which steal our time away from God. Sins are self-explanatory. One way or the other, sinful or not, entanglements take our time away from our daily spiritual priorities with God. If we become entangled in the affairs of this life, we'll find we have no time left at the end of the day to do what we need to be doing every day—spending quality time with God and with His Word.

In my book, *Be Strong! Stay Strong!*, I devote much more time and detail to these issues. In a nutshell, if we don't make time for God in prayer and Bible study, Satan will make sure there isn't any time left for God. It takes time to praise and worship God. It takes time to pray—at least if our prayers are more than just lip service to God. It takes time to cultivate an effective and meaningful prayer life. It demands discipline, hard work, and above all, time! That's why so few of us have really developed in these areas like we should.

> *You will keep him in perfect peace, whose mind is stayed on You, because he trusts in You.*
>
> —ISAIAH 26:3

God will keep us in perfect peace when our minds are focused upon Him. There's no better place to begin this than in our prayer closet! Prayer is more than just an expression of our needs, desires, and concerns. Worship is prayer. Praise is prayer. Thankfulness is prayer. All of these, when practiced consistently, bring us to a place of perfect peace. The more time we spend with God, the more His peace floods our soul, eliminates our fear, and strengthens our hands for war.

In Isaiah 26:3, the word "stayed" indicates a continuous, prolonged action. It implies a regular, habitual practice. That means perfect peace comes as we spend time with God consistently—day after day, week after week, month after month.

The challenge for most of us is in making time for God—to slow down long enough to wait upon the Lord. Many of us have the tendency to become so busy for God, we don't have any time left with God. I must constantly guard against this in my own life and ministry. The work of the ministry can become my god (idol) if I'm not careful. It can become an entanglement if I allow it to; stealing time away from the more important priorities of praise, worship, prayer, and study of the Word. If I don't watch myself daily, I'll become so busy for God's work, that all He gets from me are a few spare moments here and there throughout the day whenever I can squeeze them in. That's insulting to God, and not the way to come to a place of perfect peace.

Make Your Flesh Obey

The devil is not our only enemy. We also have to fight his world system of which he is the god (see 2 Corinthians 4:4) and our own flesh. Throughout the Word of God, we see verses that remind us of our responsibility to control and subdue our flesh. In 1 Corinthians 9:27, Paul says we must discipline our body and bring it into subjection. Our flesh must be controlled by our spirit. One day it will be recreated like our spirit man was when we were born again and acquired legal peace with God. But until God does something with our flesh, He's given us the charge to do something with it. We're to keep it under control and make it obey us.

Have you noticed that our flesh wants to do only three things in life—eat, sleep, and sin? Our flesh will never want to worship God. It will never want to praise the Lord. It will never, never, never want to get down on its knees and pray! Our flesh will fight us every step of the way. Understand that and deal with your enemy accordingly. If we don't control our flesh, our flesh will control us. It will influence our decisions and cause us to become entangled in the affairs of this life.

Each day, we have ample opportunity to neglect God and His Word. Satan comes against us directly by working through this world's system or by attempting to entice our flesh. (James 1:14-15) His purpose is to influence us, causing us to choose unwisely concerning time management. Everyone starts out with 24 hours in a day, but how we manage that time is completely up to us.

If we're going to walk in the peace of God and let it control us from the inside out, we're going to have to discipline our flesh each day to spend time with God—quality time, not just a few minutes squeezed in after all our other chores are done. God must be first place each day. In praise, worship, and prayer, spending time with God produces peace that passes all understanding! Then, that consistent, daily communion with God puts us in position to study His Word with sensitivity and effectiveness.

Yesterday's manna won't help us with today's fight of faith. We need fresh bread if we're to have the strength to stand, and having done all to stand. (Ephesians 6:13) The peace we walked in yesterday doesn't necessarily carry over into today's routine. Today is a new day, with new challenges and new opportunities to either believe God or yield to fear and worry.

For to be carnally minded is death, but to be spiritually minded is life and peace.

—ROMANS 8:6

A carnal mind is one focused upon the flesh. It is not focused upon God or things related to God and His Word. When a mind is controlled by fleshly appetites, it will ultimately lead to death. If we're being controlled by our flesh, we're being controlled indirectly by the devil. As James 1:14-15 says, he'll use our flesh to entice us to sin, which leads to death.

In context, "death" mentioned in Romans 8:6 doesn't necessarily mean physical death, or even a spiritual separation from God. This letter was written to believers—to people who had already obtained legal peace with God.

Paul is talking about the condition of being out of fellowship with God. We are still His children, but we aren't in touch with Him. We call this backsliding. "Death" could also mean a loss of anointing in ministry. It could mean that fear dominates instead of faith, for whatsoever is not of faith is sin. (Romans 14:23) Finally, it could mean that although we're children of God, God can't use us like He wants to.

The carnal Christian is still a Christian, but is the peace of God ruling and reigning in their life? According to Romans 8:6, we're talking about both the life and peace of God. There are many believers who have the life of God within them through the indwelling presence of the Holy Spirit, but they have no living peace.

But, praise God, the mind stayed upon Him is full of life and peace! The more time we spend with God—in prayer and in study of the Word—the more our hearts and minds become filled with peace. Remember 2 Corinthians 13:11, *Be of good comfort, be of one mind, live in peace; and the God of love and peace will be with you.* How do believers come to a place where we live in peace? By being of one mind! That is, our minds are stayed upon God and His Word. We're focused upon Him and Him alone. Nothing else matters but to please Him and serve Him diligently every day.

Thank God for legal peace! But it's even better to have our minds full of God's life and His peace! As the Bible says in Philippians 4:7, it's a peace which passes all understanding. Remember what Jesus said in John 16:33. It's a peace the world can't give us, and it's a peace they can't take from us. It's our Lord's peace—an extension of His very being. There is no better way to live!

Set Time Aside to Study God's Word

According to Joshua 1:8 and Psalm 1:1-3, God tells us to spend time in His Word day and night. That means His Word is to be top priority daily, right alongside our time spent in communion with Him in praise, worship, and prayer. God told us that if we did this, we would prosper and enjoy good success. Why? Because we'd be walking in perfect peace!

Start with a daily communion time with God, and from there add a consistent study of the Word of God. In Acts 6:4, church leadership gave themselves to prayer and the Word of God. They needed both to stay in peace with God and we need the same today.

Some of us are not balanced because we emphasize one at the expense of the other. People who spend all their time in prayer without equal amounts of time spent studying the Word will lack substance. On the other hand, people who spend all their time studying the Word without spending equal amounts of time in prayer will lack sensitivity and compassion. We need to be walking in living peace for God to use us, having both substance and sensitivity.

My son, do not forget my law, but let your heart keep my commands; for length of days and long life and peace they will add to you.

—PROVERBS 3:1-2

The Law and the Commandments of God refer to the Word of God. A doer of the Word will live a long and fruitful life and peace will be added in the process. As God's living peace develops in our hearts, we become more and more insulated from the opinions of others. We come to the place where we're so at peace with God and with ourselves, it doesn't matter what anyone says about us or does against us. We become free from the opinions of our peers. We also become free from the lies that Satan plants in our minds.

Now may the Lord of peace Himself give you peace always in every way.

*—*2 THESSALONIANS 3:16

God promises to give us peace always in every way. That's important, because most of us in the body of Christ are slaves to the last person who expressed an opinion about us. Dr. T. L. Osborn made that statement years ago, and I've never forgotten it. It's so true! The vast majority of Christians are guilty of this, and it's about time we all stand up and grow up. Once and for all, we need to walk in the light of who we are in Christ and be at peace with that truth. Let's allow God to take us to the place in life where His living peace protects our hearts and minds from what others think of us or say about us. In order for this to happen, we've got to renew our minds in the Word of God daily.

Great peace have those who love Your law, and nothing causes them to stumble.

*—*PSALM 119:165

In the *King James Version*, it says, *Great peace have they which love thy law: and nothing shall offend them.* The *King James Version* and the *New King James Version* use different words to say the same thing, but I prefer the *King James Version* in this instance. When we love the Word to the degree that it fills our hearts and minds, there's nothing anyone can say or do against us to cause us to stumble or get offended. To love the law means to make it first place in our lives. Along with time spent in communion with God, we're to feed our spirit man daily with His Word.

What kind of peace do we enjoy when we love the Word of God and feed upon it every day? Great peace! Not just peace, but great peace. If we really want that kind of peace manifested in our lives, we have to learn to love the Word enough to feed upon it daily as well. Aside from enjoying intimate communion with God, there is nothing more important we'll do in the course of our day.

We become like the Corinthians in 1 Corinthians 16:15. Once again from the *King James Version*, it says they addicted themselves to the ministry of the saints. They could never have done that effectively unless they had first addicted themselves to the Word of God. How can we minister effectively without basing everything we say and do upon the Bible? They were addicted. That means they needed the Word every day just to stay normal! They read the Word, studied the Word, meditated in the Word, confessed the Word, discussed the Word, believed the Word, and applied the Word.

God meant what He said in Joshua 1:8. If His Word does not depart out of our mouth (because it's in our hearts in abundance), we meditate in it day and night, and are a doer of that Word—we'll prosper and enjoy good success.

According to Psalm 1:1-3, we'll be like trees planted by rivers of water when we love the Word and feed upon it day and night. That means we'll have deep, healthy roots—the kind that are impossible to pull up and destroy. Great peace comes from feeding upon the Word every day. It will guard our hearts and minds and protect us from every attack of the enemy.

Nothing Offends Those Who Love God's Word

When God's great peace comes to us through daily feeding on the Word, we come to the place where nothing causes us to stumble, and nothing offends us anymore. Some may say that's impossible, but if God said it, then it can be accomplished. Nothing will offend us when we enjoy the great peace that comes from loving the Word enough to feed upon it daily. Not a few things or most things—but all things! We'll be so surrounded by God's great peace, bondage to the opinions of others will be a thing of the past.

No more living for the praises of men. No more riding the emotional roller coaster—up one day and down the next—all because of how others talk about us or perceive us. What a great way to live—free to serve the Lord, unencumbered by what other men think of us!

Paul had come to that place of true freedom when he wrote 1 Corinthians 4:3, *But with me it is a very small thing that I should be judged by you or by a human court.* Paul didn't care what the Corinthians thought about him, his methods, or his ministry. When he said it is a very small thing if he is judged by them, he meant their opinions were meaningless and insignificant.

Paul knew he wasn't in Corinth because the Corinthians asked him to come or asked him to stay. His decision to come was based upon the leading of the Lord, and his decision to stay or to leave would also be based upon that same leading. As far as Paul was concerned, what the Corinthian church thought of him was a non-issue.

Paul wasn't planning to stay in Corinth because they loved all of his messages and bought all of his products, books, and resource materials. He wasn't planning to stay because he knew they liked his style of ministry. If they liked him and his ministry, that was fine. But if they didn't like him and his ministry, that was still fine too! It's what the Lord said to him about his work in Corinth—that's what counted to Paul, nothing else. In other words, he had living peace about who he was, where he was, and what he was doing there. He would stay as long as God wanted Him to stay, no matter what anyone in the Corinthian church thought about it. According to Psalm 119:165, that's the kind of peace we can have when we love the Word of God and feed upon it daily.

And let the peace of God rule in your hearts, to which also you were called in one body, and be thankful. Let the word of Christ dwell in you richly in all wisdom.

—COLOSSIANS 3:15-16

When the peace of God rules in our lives, it's because we let the word of Christ dwell in us richly. There are two key parts to that statement. First, we must let the Word dominate. That's an act of our free will. The Bible doesn't jump off the shelf into our lap, open itself up, and read to us. We have to decide to set time aside for God's Word. It's as simple as that. Second, the Word must dwell richly within us. That means our time spent in the Word must be significant. Dwelling in us richly does not mean we read the Word once every four days for 20 minutes in between our favorite TV programs. It doesn't mean we just follow somebody's "read-the-Bible-through-in-a-year" program. It doesn't mean we do everything else first, and then if we've got time left at the end of the day, we read our Bible.

If we're going to walk in living peace, the Word must dwell in us richly. It must abound within our hearts, for out of the abundance of our heart the mouth will speak. (Matthew 12:34) We're not talking about an occasional glance at our Bible or reading it only when we show up at church on Sunday mornings. If we want to come to the place where we walk above our problems, we're going to have to spend the time necessary in the Word. There is no substitute for spending significant amounts of time in the Word. It's what gives us the peace which makes walking above problems possible.

> *Oh, that you had heeded My commandments! Then your peace would have been like a river, and your righteousness like the waves of the sea.*

—Isaiah 48:18

To heed means to pay attention to and obey. If we pay attention to and obey God's Word, our peace will be like a river. It will be a continuous refreshing in our lives. But if we fail to let the Word dwell in us richly, we'll have no one to blame for our mediocrity but ourselves.

Why are so many of us enjoying legal peace with God but failing to enjoy His living peace? Because many of us today are like the Jews to whom God made this statement in Isaiah. We're not heeding God's Word. We're not making it a priority every day. Giving ourselves to the Word continuously will bring God's peace like a mighty river into our hearts, minds, ministries, and lives.

Jesus said that He left us His peace to enjoy and use. Are you enjoying it, and are you using it? The choice is yours to make, so make the right choice!

Pursue Peace

> *Flee also youthful lusts; but pursue righteousness, faith, love, peace with those who call on the Lord out of a pure heart.*

—2 Timothy 2:22

Let him turn away from evil and do good; Let Him seek peace and pursue it.

—1 PETER 3:11

Both of these passages were written to people already born again. People who already had acquired legal peace with God were told to pursue peace. In other words, they were told to aggressively take the next step and let God's living peace dominate their lives and ministries.

For the kingdom of God is not eating and drinking, but righteousness and peace and joy in the Holy Spirit. . . . Therefore let us pursue the things which make for peace and the things by which one may edify another.

—ROMANS 14:17,19

The Word says we should be pursuing the things which make for peace. We are to aggressively work towards establishing a daily routine which guarantees quality time with God and His Word. But remember, it's not going to happen just because God wants it to happen. It's not going to happen just because it needs to happen. It's going to happen when we want it to happen and not a moment before. When we begin to pursue peace because it's a top priority in our lives, we'll begin to see the power of peace in our lives.

The Word of God tells us to love the Lord our God with all our heart, our mind, our soul, and our strength. (Mark 12:30) Pursuing peace requires the same kind of total commitment. We must go after this with all our being—it can't be an afterthought or a passing issue. It's got to become a priority for the rest of our lives.

Living peace is available. We can have living peace. We can walk in the light of it. But we have to pursue it. The gift of peace has been given to us, but we have to cultivate it. We have to devote our time and energies to it. We have to decide living peace is important and make the decision to go after it wholeheartedly.

I'm going after peace in my life and I challenge you to do it in yours!

Let these marvelous truths
Bring peace to your heart.
They are gifts to you from God,
So they are yours—
Now and forevermore.

I will lift up my eyes to the hills—from whence comes my help?

My help comes from the Lord, Who made heaven and earth.

He will not allow your foot to be moved; He who keeps you will not slumber.

Behold, He who keeps Israel shall neither slumber nor sleep.

The Lord is your keeper; the Lord is your shade at your right hand.

The sun shall not strike you by day, nor the moon by night.

The Lord shall preserve you from all evil; He shall preserve your soul.

The Lord shall preserve your going out and your coming in from this time forth, and even forevermore.

—PSALM 121

What then shall we say to these things? If God is for us, who can be against us?

He who did not spare His own Son, but delivered Him up for us all, how shall He not with Him also freely give us all things?

Who shall bring a charge against God's elect? It is God who justifies.

Who is he who condemns? It is Christ who died, and furthermore is also risen, who is even at the right hand of God, who also makes intercession for us.

Who shall separate us from the love of Christ? Shall tribulation, or distress, or persecution, or famine, or nakedness, or peril, or sword?

As it is written:

"For Your sake we are killed all day long; We are accounted as sheep for the slaughter."

Yet in all these things we are more than conquerors through Him who loved us.

For I am persuaded that neither death nor life, nor angels nor principalities nor powers, nor things present nor things to come,

nor height nor depth, nor any other created thing, shall be able to separate us from the love of God which is in Christ Jesus our Lord.

—ROMANS 8:31-39

Peace be to you,

Peace be to your family,

Peace be to your household,

And peace be to all you have!

God bless you!

REV. MIKE KEYES SR.

PRAYER OF SALVATION

If you've never received Jesus as Lord and Savior, you can do that right now, wherever you are—and you don't need anyone with you to do this. Even if you're by yourself, you can pray the prayer below from your heart, out loud to the Lord, and receive the free gift of eternal salvation. Jesus stands at the door to every man's heart and knocks, but only we can open the door (Rev. 3:20). The Bible says with the heart we believe and with the mouth we confess our salvation (Rom. 10:9,10). Right now, therefore, lift your heart and voice to the Lord and pray this prayer:

Dear Lord Jesus, I believe that You are the Son of God and that You died on a cross, paid for my sins, and rose from the dead. Therefore, right now, I open the door to my heart, and I choose to make You the Lord of my life. I confess You as my Lord and personal Savior, and I ask You to come into my heart now. I repent of all my sins, receive my forgiveness, and accept You as the Lord and Savior of my life—for the rest of my life. From this day forward, I will live for You and You alone, my Lord Jesus. Thank You, Lord, for loving me and for saving my soul. Amen.

If you prayed that simple prayer sincerely from the heart, the Lord has heard you and done exactly what you have asked. The Holy Spirit has come and recreated your spirit man on the inside, and you are now a born-again child of God (John 3:3). This is the greatest miracle anyone can receive, and it happened because of your faith! You're saved now, not because of how you feel after you prayed but because of the choice you made before you prayed! You made a decision, and your salvation is based upon that decision. You reached out and chose to receive the free gift of salvation by making Jesus Lord of your life (John 1:12; Rom. 5:17). Congratulations!

Please contact me, and share the good news about your decision today to make Jesus the Lord of your life. All of heaven rejoices with you and for you (Matt. 18:12-14), and I'm so very proud of you!

REVEREND MIKE KEYES, SR.

ABOUT THE AUTHOR

Mike Keyes grew up in Ohio and was raised in the Roman Catholic church. In 1973, he graduated from college to become a successful advertising executive and graphic artist. On September 21, 1978, at age twenty-six, he was born again and Spirit filled two days later. Immediately, the gifts of the Spirit began working in his life. Through his local church, he began to witness on the streets, in area prisons, and anywhere he could hand out tracts.

In September 1979, Reverend Keyes resigned his job to attend Rhema Bible Training Center in Tulsa, Oklahoma, graduating in May 1980. In September 1980, he traveled to the Philippines with a one-way plane ticket, arriving without knowledge of the language or customs and with no one there to meet him. When he got off that plane to begin his ministry, he had twenty dollars in his pocket, one footlocker containing his Bible, class notes, a few changes of clothing, and the promise of support totaling $250 from no one except his parents and one small church in Toledo, Ohio.

From those humble beginnings and through his faithfulness to the calling of God over the years, the Lord has used Reverend Keyes extensively to reach untold numbers of people in the Philippines and around the world. Always emphasizing outreach to the remote, overlooked, out-of-the-way villages and towns that no one else has gone to, at the thirty-year anniversary of his ministry work in September 2010, it is conservatively estimated that over one-half million souls have been won to Christ in his nationwide crusades in the Philippines.

Mike Keyes Ministries International (MKMI) is an apostolic ministry that reaches the lost, teaches the Christians, and trains the ministers. With a consistent crusade outreach, a church network of hundreds of churches, and a two-year Bible school; Revered Keyes and his staff, pastors, graduates, and students continue to fulfill the Great Commission wherever he is instructed to go by the Holy Spirit—throughout the Philippines and around the world.

Reverend Keyes is married to a native Filipina, Ethel, and has two children.

For additional information:
- About Reverend Keyes and the MKMI ministry
- About becoming involved in prayer or financial support
- About participating in our annual missions tour
- About obtaining more copies of this book or other books and CD teaching sets

Please contact us at:
- Web: www.mkmi.org
- E-mail: ekeyes@mkmi.org